Laid out with ta
and judgement

The landscape, architecture
and social history of

THE PARK

and its environs in

CHELTENHAM

Aylwin Sampson

**PALLAS
PRESS**

University of Gloucestershire

2010

foreword

SIR HENRY ELWES KCVO
HM LORD-LIEUTENANT OF GLOUCESTERSHIRE
1992 - 2010

THE PARK TO the South of Cheltenham is an area known to many but not fully appreciated by everyone as they drive through. Aylwin Sampson's book now gives us the opportunity to meander through one of Gloucestershire's gems.

We are fortunate in the county in having a number of outstandingly attractive locations and Regency Cheltenham is certainly one of them. Aylwin's diligent research has now given us a fascinating record of the principal houses of this area, their architectural distinction and the social history of them and their surroundings.

The development in the nineteenth century was not without its difficulties and these are well illustrated in this book. The History of false starts, interruptions and eventual success, show how fortunate we are that The Park has survived as an outstanding area of architectural and horticultural interest.

St. Mary's College first used The Park for higher education purposes in the 1930's. Since that time, The Park has been home to students, and is today a campus of the University of Gloucestershire. The University has added to the stock of distinguished buildings on the site, winning awards for architectural merit for a number of new buildings.

An area with as rich a history as The Park is fortunate in having residents and occupiers who see themselves as custodians of a proud tradition. With a 24 acre park, a collection of magnificent specimen trees and its distinguished architectural features, The Park continues to be an area 'laid out with taste and judgement.' I hope you enjoy reading something of its fascinating history.

An important and most elegant improvement has of late been made in the appearance of the south side of the town by the laying out of about 100 acres of land, the property of Thomas Billings, esq., solicitor, denominated 'The Park Estate' ... arranged by the proprietor agreeably to a design entirely his own, and on a plan altogether original.

The principal attraction is a handsome circular drive... enclosing an area called "The Park" twenty acres of which have been recently purchased for the purpose of forming zoological and botanical gardens on a scale superior to that of any similar provincial establishments in the kingdom.

The chief object seems to have been to afford sites for detached villas combining the splendour of the town with the charms and beauties of the country... How far he has succeeded in the bold undertaking is demonstrated by the number of mansions occupied by some of the most wealthy and fashionable residents in Cheltenham.

GRIFFITHS *History of Cheltenham* 1838

Preface

THE IMPETUS FOR this account of The Park came from a talk at The Park Area Residents Community annual general meeting in March 2004, followed by a repeat to the Gloucestershire Landscape and Gardens Trust. Both revealed a strong interest in this aspect of Cheltenham and, as the second talk was open to members of the University – both events incidentally held at The Park campus – there was evidence of support and commitment to taking the idea forward.

It so happened that a group of residents had been compiling a history of Tivoli Road and there was already a publication on Tivoli; the University had commissioned a feasibility report on the Campus Lake, which included a basic history of The Park; while a pamphlet including information on the historic buildings of the College of Higher Education had been in existence since 1991.

Consequently all seemed propitious to approach the University with a view to producing a history, not only of The Park, but also of the feeder roads which were integral to the area's development. Appropriately, it was the University's Business School which agreed to support the project and to collaborate in its publication, and the partnership beginning at the start of 2005 has come to a fruition that it is hoped does justice to an important part of Cheltenham's history.

The compilation of an account such as this owes much to the help of a wide range of persons and documents. It would be inordinate to name every one, but niggardly to name only a handful. So, risking the charges of partiality or negligence, the catalogue below will at least recognise the contribution of all.

Householders: Albert Ashton, Michael Bartosch, Peter Bassett, Eric Bayliss, Susan Blanchfield, Sheila Bloom, Martin Boothman, George Breeze, Bryan Davies, Matthew Gemmill, Elizabeth Gobourn, David Harding, Robin Harrod, James Hawtin, Trevor Hill, Edgar Huber, Pamela Jackson, Michael James, Bruce Maughfling, Colin Mort, Michael Parker, Johanna Peebles, Michael Phillips, Anthony Pick, Shelagh Powys-Hancox, Iona Radice, Nina Reeves, Toby Roberts, Peter Rogers, Derek Rowles, Patrick

Sanderson, Ralph Settatree, Mark Silva, Rodger Smith, David Stevens, Nicholas Thorne, Keith Todd, James Tyrrell, Julian Tyson-Woodcock, Peter Vaus, Muriel Waldron, Ralph Wilkins, Eric Woodhead.

The 'road historians': Jill Barlow (Tivoli), Brian Torode (St. Stephen's)

Directories: I. G. Tracey

Reference material: Steven Blake, Elaine Heasman, James Hodsdon, Geoff North, Ken Pollock

Botanic illustration and listing: Michael Hickey

House Agents: Peter Ball, Humberts, Knight Frank, Charles Lear, Read Maurice

Landscape Architects: Mitchell Harris Partnership

University Archives: Lorna Scott, Caro McIntosh

The University of Gloucestershire Business School: Barry Davies

A.S. Cheltenham, 2010

Contents

KEY TO THE PROPERTY ENTRIES

(a) Statutory List *(SL)*, Local List *(LL)*, **number, name(s)**, dates, reason

(b) Date of building, architect, builder, cost

(c) * Census or ** Electoral list/Date of ownership/occupancy

(d) Architectural features, date of significant structural changes

(e) Date of change of use

(f) Boundary and garden features

(g) Brief biography of notable owners/occupants

(h) Significant events

It should be noted that the listing of names relating to each building is taken from a selective sampling of directories and, because many properties were leased for temporary use during the 'season' or as a home for expatriates overseas while sons were at school in the town, their status may be as owner or occupier. Further, the succession of male by female name may indicate the former's absence abroad and not his death. The unofficial designating "Mrs Colonel" was a 19th century social convention for widows of army officers holding that rank. And, finally, the date accompanying the name is derived from the year of the directory consulted and may, therefore, not represent the exact beginning of the person's ownership or occupancy.

the Park

I T WAS CHELTENHAM'S good fortune to be a late-comer to the era of spas; fortunate because by the beginning of the 19th century the patronage of the aristocracy had given place to the emergence of what can be called 'polite society'; fortunate that a leading element in that society was the attorney; and fortunate that members of that profession were, through their involvement with property and land transactions, attracted to engage in land speculation themselves. Add to this the conjunction of a period when domestic architecture was at its most elegant with the Regency villa set in its generous plot, with the social habits of promenading in the leafy open air after taking the waters, thus a fashionable 'garden town' was the happy result.

For Cheltenham a comparison between two such speculations illustrates the point. Pittville owes its genesis to Joseph Pitt, a lawyer, buying in 1806 an area of 253 acres, north of the town and devising a scheme, 1824-30, for 100 acres of walks, lake, with a spa and 500-600 houses; in 1825 Thomas Billings, a lawyer too, buying 100 acres south of the town in the manor of Leckhampton, reselling to a Society, specially formed to develop twenty acres as a park for botanical, horticulture and zoological use, a lake and forty three houses. Both men employ architects: Pitt, John Forbes; Billings, Samuel Daukes. And a spa too is established by Billings in 1850. In 1841 the Park enterprise is abandoned and the land sold to Daukes; a year later Pitt dies, owing £50,000. Such was the precarious nature of these speculations; and fortuitous that both survive today largely intact.

The Park Estate comprises part of the medieval manor of Leckhampton with its field boundaries overlaid, and determined, by natural features. On the north, Westal Brook created ponds and lakes like Virginia Water, while on the west, Moorend Stream and Hatherley Brook joined to provide another acqueous boundary. With a substratum of clay interrupted by two salients of sand running north-south centred on Moorend Park Road and, further west, Kidnappers Lane, the "campus" lake's position was dependent on "a spring of water running from Moor End Grove to, or through the

Estate" (1841 Auction details). Moreover it is interesting to note that the pre-Billings field boundaries appear to ignore the presence of this campus lake, for the south-west edge of the Mowing Breach cuts neatly in half the present lake.

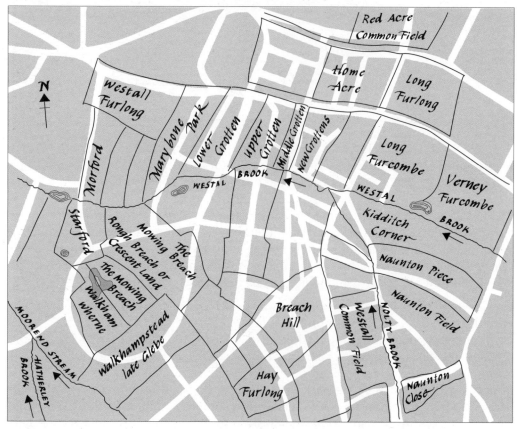

The road pattern of The Park and surrounding area superimposed on the field system existing before development in the 19th century.

Merrett's 1834 map shows the Park has been converted from a medieval field system in the north Leckhampton parish to an enclosed area; divided into a major treed part containing a serpentine road leading to a proposed – but never built – structure connected by another serpentine path to the lake, as well as by another straight avenue to an entrance gate opposite Moorend Park Road. Intriguingly the disposition of trees in the west area, skirting the lake, has led to a conjecture that this may be the vestigial evidence of a medieval 'portway' linking Cheltenham via what is now Lypiatt Road and Tivoli Lane to Leckhampton village.

Map by Henry Merrett 1834 clearly shows the distinctive pear shape of The Park at the southern extremity of the town.

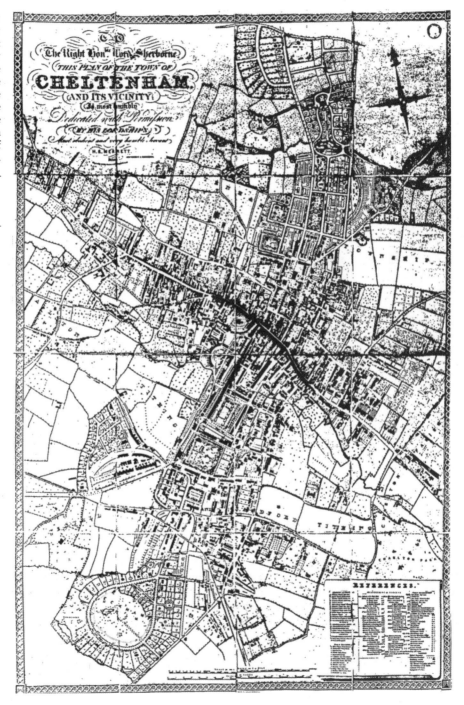

The date of Merrett's map indicates the beginning of the Billings 'era'. For in 1825 he, Thomas Billings, a solicitor, together with Arthur Parker, a builder, bought some 110 acres for £3,220 comprising the Park Estate from Henry Norwood Trye, Lord of the Manor of Leckhampon. The project was ambitious, as Griffiths describes in his *History of Cheltenham*, 1838, "The chief object seems to have been to afford sites for ... a class of houses ... combining the splendour of the town with the charms and beauties of the country ... expending a very considerable sum in the ... drives, promenades and grounds which are now in their full tide of beauty." Not the least important was the establishment of zoological and botanic gardens together with a museum of natural history in the 22 acres within the pear-shape which included a proposed crescent of villas and at the 'sharp end' looking down Park Place, a pleasure ground, doubtless for private or public enjoyment on payment of a subscription.

The configuration of The Park is markedly east west, and this orientation survives in the map accompanying the prospectus for its sale in 1833. Also evident is the emphatic entrance avenue to the south.

The purchaser of The Park area, excluding the Pleasure Ground and Crescent to the east, was the Gloucester Zoological, Botanical and Horticultural Society, a joint stock company formed for this specific area by the Cheltenham Floral and Horticultural Society and the Literary and Philosophical Institution. Billings himself had laid out the perimeter drive and the pleasure grounds according to Griffiths' History 1838, opening at the North Lodge a "subscription book towards the heavy expense of ... repair", but his involvement with The Park's development continued, indeed became more significant. For the Zoological, Botanical and Horticultural Society had been persuaded to hold a competition for designing a layout. Under a pseudonym of 'Perseverando' Billings was adjudged the winner, awarded the fifty guineas prize, and after his donating it to the society "reserved to himself the power of directing in what manner it should be applied"! Indeed, he also kept ownership of the roads in the area, thereby receiving rentals too.

So Billings succeeded in having his layout implemented, and at no cost to himself. The Society issued 4000 shares at £5, thus realising some £20,000, and it would need every penny of that, for Billings's design was ambitious to the point of absurdity. Some elements of his design were praised, in particular "the idea of forming the Botanic Garden so as to assimilate in shape with the Northern and Southern hemispheres of our globe in the extreme, and cannot fail to afford much amusement and instruction to the lovers of geographical and botanical research; more particularly as it is intended to cultivate in the different quarters those plants which flourish in the various latitudes. This arrangement it is thought will be of great use to the junior members of families" (Griffiths *History of Cheltenham*, 1838). Bisected by the Grand Promenade 750 feet long, stretching from the Grand Terrace holding the Conservatory, the grounds to the south

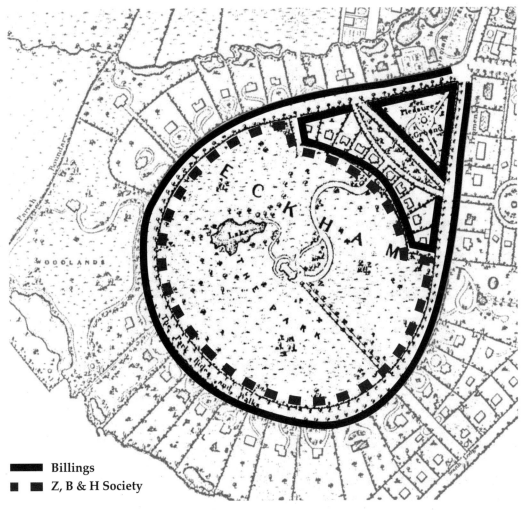

▬▬▬ Billings
■   ■ Z, B & H Society

An enlargement of Merrett's map, 1834: the demarcation of the area bought by the Zoological Botanical & Horticultural Society and the part that Billings retained can be identified; the avenue of trees on an axis with Moorend Park road ends with a proposed building to occupy a central position linked by serpentine paths to the lake, and a crescent of villas.

were to have large botanical gardens planted in the shape of the Continents as Griffiths states with their indigenous specimens, a labyrinth, aviaries for rapacious birds, eagle house, and even a bear pit, all linked by serpentine walks.

However it is the area north of the Promenade, (known now as the Elephant Walk), which was to exhibit a more rustic character – despite enclosures for rhinoceros, buffalos and elephant. For here the lake was to be deepened and extended northwards, creating the two islands for otters and beavers and linked to the land by a rustic bridge, presumably to afford access for the proposed hermit!

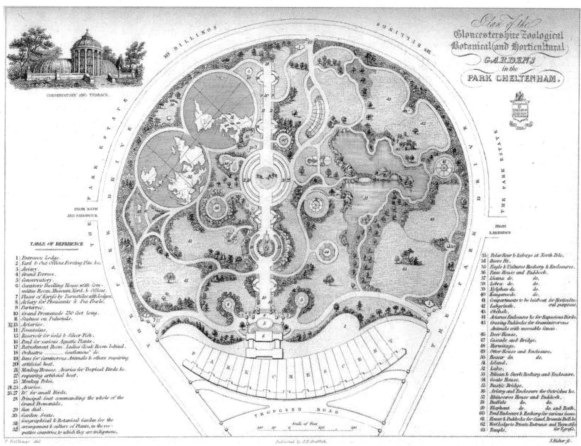

This engraving by J Fisher published by S.Y Griffiths, owner/editor of the *Cheltenham Chronicle* in 1828 and purchaser of the Queen's Hotel in 1840, is undated. As it bears a shield with the words 'designed by Billings, solicitor, Cheltenham' it cannot be his entry for the Zoological, Botanical and Horticultural Society's competition, but was probably a more "finished presentation" to attract shareholders, even perhaps adding exhibits.

How much was translated into reality is difficult to establish: the Elephant Walk and the islanded lake survive, but whether the north entrance with its imposing lodge designed by S. W. Daukes has suffered more than that building's demolition, or if the present 'fives court' represents the exact area of the paddocks for "graminiverous animals with moveable fences" remain uncertain.

All we can learn, from such sources as *Cheltenham Looker-On*, is that

> "the Zoological Gardens have within the last six weeks made rapid progress. A large portion of the lake has been excavated and many of the surrounding walks and embankments completely formed, and the planting is now proceeded with from the entrance up to the proposed conservatories, and on either side of the Grand Promenade … The committee of management will be able to give an account of their stewardship as cannot fail satisfying the subscribers." (25 Nov. 1837)

The formal opening of the Zoological Gardens on 28th of June 1838 was unusually eventful, and is worth recounting fully being part of the town's celebration of Queen Victoria's Coronation Day. In the morning after services at the parish church and St. Pauls, followed by a public breakfast at Montpellier Spa,

> "the company rose, and the trustees and committee of the Zoological Society, with the Council of the Literary Institution, moved into the Promenade Walk, and formed themselves into line for the purpose of proceeding to open the Zoological Gardens. The following is the order of procession:
>
> Standard Bearer with the Royal Standard, The Montpellier Band, The Trustees of the Garden, H. Trye, Esq, Pearson Thompson, Esq, Council of the Literary Institution, President and Vice President of the Literary Institution, Dr. Boisragon, Dr Conolly, Committee of Management, Horticultural Committee, Shareholders and Subscribers, Train of Carriages - the ladies of the party.
>
> The procession proceeded through Suffolk Square and Park Place to the Gardens, the Gates of which, on its arrival opposite the Lodge, were thrown open. As the party crossed the entrance, the signal was given, and a royal salute commenced firing, and continued until the full complement of one-and-twenty guns had been discharged, while the company advanced up the main approach to the terrace, and through the Floral And Horticultural Exhibition which was there arranged under two spacious marquees provided for that especial purpose. The crowd which thronged the tents during the whole of the day was so great, that it was quite impossible to examine, with any very scrutinizing eye, the various groups of fruits and flowers which covered the different stands; but a mere glance was sufficient to convey to the mind, among which the cactuses and heaths appeared predominantly the grapes and strawberries, and the vegetables throughout, reflected great credit upon their respective growers.

Immediately following the "officials" of the procession, the company, subscribers and non-subscribers, began to flow in, and so continued in one unbroken stream throughout the remainder of the afternoon. The beauty of the Gardens, the fineness of the day, the fragrance of the Floral Show, and the music of the Band, all contributed to render the scene one of surpassing gaiety and animation. On all sides we heard the warmest expressions of delight, admiration, and surprise, for all appeared equally struck with the wonders which art, guided by correct taste and competent skill, has been able to achieve in the short space which had elapsed since the Gardens had been commenced. The recollection of the level field was still fresh in the memory, and the mind, when called upon to contemplate the scene before it, almost doubted whether or not the days of Aladdin and enchantment had not again returned." (*Looker-On* 30 June, 1838)

The main entrance with Daukes' Italianate Lodge housing "a small ornithological museum of numerous specimens of British and Foreign birds"; beyond the gates stands a structure which might have been one of the many aviaries proposed by Billings.

In the afternoon it was the turn of some 3,000 children to consume roast beef and plum pudding in the Market House, while the 200 adults were similarly fed in the courtyard of the Queens Hotel. At 3.30 o'clock they all formed up to march, accompanied by "an immense number of people" to the Gardens via Park Place.

"On the arrival of the procession at the Gardens, a sad scene of confusion took place, the crowd being here so great that it was found for some time impossible to force a way through, and the utmost exertions of the committee, as well as of the friends and servants of the society, were put into requisition to accomplish this object. The children were, however, at length got in, though in broken detachments, and a heavy shower of rain coming fortunately on, the pressure from without was lightened, and the throng became consequently more manageable. Happily no accident occurred, though very serious consequences were at one time apprehended. The rain was of short continuance, and the schools, once safely within the gates, paraded quietly and at leisure through the Gardens, and enjoyed as best they could the scene and objects around them, until nearly six o'clock, by which time most of them had left the ground. It was found impossible to form into any regular line of procession for the return, and each school therefore took its own homeward course, and thus encountered less difficulty in proceeding through the crowded streets." (ibid)

So ended in some disarray the Gardens' opening, and a day that had begun so promisingly. Perhaps it symbolized, too, the future fortunes of the enterprise itself.

Let us hope the subscribers were optimists, for there were dark clouds looming literally when annual Floral and Horticultural Exhibitions suffered bad attendance. Of particular note was the Fourth which was as

"equally unfortunate as its predecessor with the weather, in respect of distance from the town and want of shelter and adequate accommodation unfit the zoological Gardens for combating against the disadvantages of wind and rain. The consequence was that the attendance proved unusually thin, nor was the show itself very crowded with specimens" (*Looker-On* 27 July 1839)

and indeed, such ominous descriptions as in Davies' *Visitor's Handbook* 1840:

"though in their zoological character [of] moderate pretensions [with an] extensive water and a picturesque rockery at the outlet of the lake, public support has been wholly inadequate [though the] charge for admission for non-subscribers is one shilling each."

For it seems the foliage of plantations, and the "sweet perfume of a thousand flowers" proved less of an attraction than a young monkey. (*Looker-On* 30 May 1840)

Small wonder then that the following subsequently appeared in the *Looker-On*:

"Zoological and Botanical Gardens are advertised for sale at the Auction Mart, next Friday... There appears no probability of rescue of these very beautiful grounds, which since their formation have constituted a feature of peculiar attraction in the estimation of our summer visitors, being saved from the auctioneer's hammer. We believe the income of the Gardens has never equalled the expenditure necessary to keep them up, and from the small measure of support accorded them by the inhabitants generally. There seemed no reasonable hope of this ever proving the case." (24 April 1841)

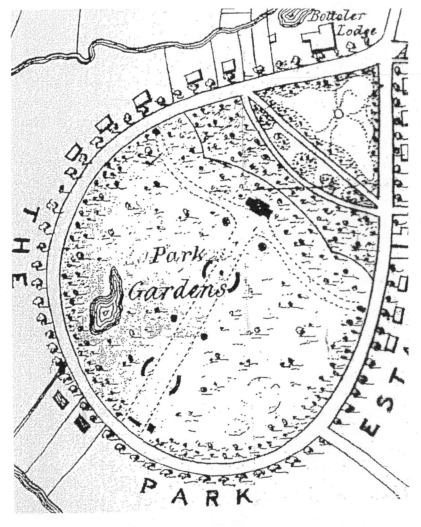

1843 map indicating the change to a pleasure garden: the avenue aligned to Moorend Park Road marked on Merretts map has gone together with a projected building at a serpentine path; the Grand Promenade/Elephant Walk is suggested, but the main North Entrace has been omitted except for a meagre building presumably the Lodge; but the emphatic structure in the axial position bears little relation to what was built, while the perimeter trees are now shown within the park boundary.

Rescue however did arrive in the person of Samuel Whitfield Daukes, an architect who had already designed the main entrance lodge, free of charge. His other works in Cheltenham included Lansdown railway station, St Peter's Church and St Paul's College now Francis Close Hall. Regrettably his own house, Tudor Lodge, only survives as a name and a solitary pier on the east perimeter of The Park. The twenty acres now took on a new role: that of a public pleasure ground, Still divided by the Grand Promenade, the halves developed distinct characteristics: that on the south east became a sports area, while the other north west retained the woodland, rustic identity.

The *Looker-On* expressed it thus on 4 June 1842

"The Park Gardens having passed into fresh hands [i.e. Daukes] and undergone many important alterations to adapt them to other purposes ... are about to re-open and become the scene of amusements of a novel character ... it is intended to introduce a series of Pic-Nic Entertainments. These if properly conducted and favoured with fine weather may be rendered delightful sources of enjoyment and recreation."

And in an advertisement,

"[The Park Gardens] will be opened from eight in the morning till sun-set daily, Sundays excepted... the extensive ground on the east side has been laid down for Archery, Cricket, Bowling and other games for which separate clubs may be formed, and in proportion to the support given Tennis, Racket and Fives courts will be erected behind the (Grand) Terrace on which a permanent shelter will be provided ... The County of Gloucester Archery & Cricket Club proposes having the exclusive right of the cricket and archery ground two days per week.

Admission: Family subscription £1/11/6; Single subscription 15/-; Single admission 6d."

On the north west half, the fourteen acres included "promenades, lawns, ... flower beds, clumps of choicest shrubs ... and a beautiful sheet of water having a romantic little rockery at the lower end." (Davies' *View of Cheltenham* 4th edn. 1843)

But again foreboding storm clouds gathered. Or as the *Looker-On* put it,

"The Cheltenham & Gloucestershire Cricket Club appears not unlikely to be deprived of its excellent ground in the Park Gardens which are to be shortly sold for building purposes ... some arrangements for preserving this well laid-out ground could be entered into by which those portions of the Gardens might be reserved." (27 January 1844)

So ended such occasions as these sporting events and galas like the gypsy, reported in *The Examiner* on 15 June 1842:

"This novel affair came off on Monday afternoon under the superintendence of Mr Morgan who rented the Garden for the occasion. The company consisted of between two and three hundred persons and the amusements consisted of dancing etc. A quadrille band was in attendance and the "dance of the green" was kept up with spirit and animation until near 10 o'clock. Refreshments were provided at a modest charge by Mrs Waterfall. One cannot fail to record attention to the delightful gardens which only require to be better known and more extensively patronised. The alterations and improvements which have been made in the last few months have very much added to the enchantment of the spot and the 'tout ensemble' on Monday evening, the beauty of the scenery, the gay strains of music, the merry laughter of the company and the happy groups tripping the light fantastic to their hearts' content, will cause the gypsy gala long to dwell in the memory of those present."

From portions of the 1855 Town Plan. The winding paths around the lake (some surviving) and the Grand Promenade culminating in the Terrace can be identified.

And the gala on the 6th September 1843, which had ominous words

"Mr Cyngell's gala at the Park Garden on Friday evening drew together a tolerably numerous company to that delightful spot. The amusements were varied and appear to afford satisfaction to those present. A display of fireworks and Mr Cyngell's ascent over the lake concluded the entertainment for the evening",

and even after the auction of the land in 1844, a Pigeon Match in 1849.

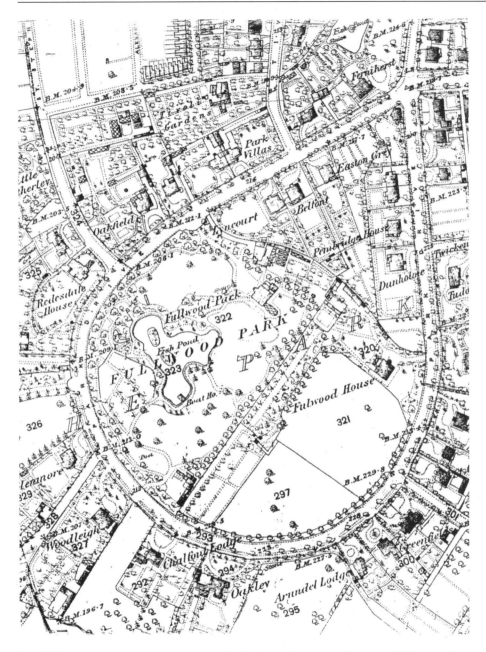

This 1887 map gives a detailed delineation of the boundary between Fullwood and Fulwood, the layout of the villas' gardens, the paths around the lake, and the planting along the perimeter.

The purchaser of the Gardens in 1844 was Andrew Taylor responding to a sales offer which extolled the merits of the estate and describing the twenty acres with such terms as "disposed with great taste" and containing "splendid walks" encircled by "beautiful residences" suitable for the erecting of a large mansion or villas and even suggesting its potential as a cemetery!

Sale particulars January 1844: designation as Fullwood Park is absent, while the suggested development includes that of a cemetery; the Grand Promenade, "splendid walks", and cricket ground should be noted.

PARTICULARS.

THE VERY VALUABLE FREEHOLD PROPERTY,

lately known as

THE ZOOLOGICAL GARDENS,

in the Parish of Leckhampton, but considered as part of

THE TOWN OF CHELTENHAM,

Surrounded by the Park Drives and Promenades of 60 feet wide, and a Circle of Beautiful Residences,

Containing about Twenty Acres,

and forming one of the most delightful situations for either

A LARGE MANSION, OR DETACHED VILLAS,

OR FOR A CEMETERY;

ABOUT TWELVE ACRES ARE DISPOSED WITH GREAT TASTE,

AND LAID OUT IN SPLENDID WALKS,

Ornamented with Shrubberies, Flower Beds, undulating Lawns, and

AN EXTENSIVE LAKE,

making together a most beautiful GARDEN, the approach to which is by a

HANDSOME LODGE, IN THE CHARACTER OF AN ITALIAN VILLA,

A TERRACE WALK,

and

GRAND PROMENADE, UPWARDS OF 750 FEET IN EXTENT,

And Forty Feet in Width;

IN THE REAR OF THIS ARE ABOUT EIGHT ACRES OF LAND,

heretofore used as a Cricket Ground and Kitchen Garden,

in which are some

CHOICE FRUIT TREES.

THE ESTATE IS PRINCIPALLY ENCLOSED BY AN ORNAMENTAL WOODEN FENCING,

And a Wall nearly 300 yards in extent.

THE FENCING AND WALL WILL BE INCLUDED IN THE SALE.

THIS PROPERTY HAS COST MANY THOUSAND POUNDS IN ITS FORMATION,

it has in itself an abundant supply of Spring Water,

and is acknowledged

as one of

The most enviable Situations in Cheltenham.

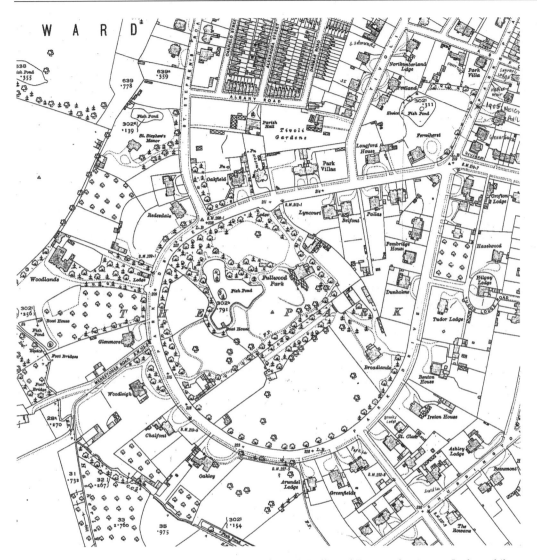

A map later than 1887's showing development within the Park; Fullwood Entrance has its new Lodge, while the house itself has the Solarium; Fulwood is now Broadlands and there is its own Lodge opposite Oakley; the presence of the pair of houses east of the former Easton Grey now Pallas shows it to be after 1897; and the creation of houses at the junction of Moorend Park Road and Shurdington Road - Park Grange later Moorend Park Hotel - suggest a date around 1920.

In the event Andrew Taylor sold the site ten years later to "James Gilbertson of Oakland Park, Weybridge for the purpose of erecting thereon a mansion suitable for his own residence" (*Looker-On* 19 Nov 1854) This resulted in the division, evident on subsequent maps, between Fullwood Park and Fulwood House (now Broadlands). Fullwood Park had the arcadian glades, shrubberies and the lake with its islands, and rockwork where back in 1842, after a cricket match, "a Welsh harpist was stationed to accompany the Lancashire Hand-Bell Ringers performing in the Terrace of the Grand Promenade, before the Firework Display." Incidentally it is intriguing that a feature that is present in the Billings design, the Cascade, still appears on the 1855 map, at the north west edge of the lake linked to a boomerang-shape pool, though the Hermitage nearby also on the Billings design has gone. The Grand Promenade (Elephant Walk) itself was appropriated by Fulwood (Broadlands), to be abbreviated by kitchen gardens and an orchard at its western end.

This presentation by Samuel Daukes has significant features and is worth scrutiny. The map shows the 'sharp end' of The Park, with its pleasure ground of Billings, before the introduction of his Park Spa at the junction of Park Place and Argyle Place / Grafton road. All the houses whether planned or built include Virginia Water / Boteler / Fernihurst whose facade is shown at the top. Two of the many lakes owing their location to the Westall Brook front the house and the balustrade marks the culverted water below Park Place. The fountain depicted in the further lake also features on the map.

On the eastern side of the road the bow fronts of Segrave House / Mercian Court can be identified.

At the bottom of the sheet is a view looking north; the two classical temples are also shown on the map's boundary and are called North Lodges. One of them was removed in 1850 to serve as Park Spa.

A "spa interlude" is worth interpolating at this point. In 1850 the *Looker-On* reported "a new spa with excellent saline water at the opposite end of Park Place … a little classical lodge has been removed near Segrave Villas [now Mercian Court] and converted into a Pump Room." (20 July)

The location of this fortuitous discovery was on the five acres of land retained by Billings at the sale in 1835. He engaged Samuel Bendhall to investigate, using his forty years experience at the Montpellier Spa, and indeed granting him the lease. Bendhall seems to have been alert to the potential for he not only offered subscriptions for use of the spa, 1 guinea for a family for the season, ½ guinea for a single person, but also secured admission to the walks or drives for ½ guinea, 5 shillings walks only, and 7/6 using a wheel chair! This building was later replaced by Cornerways, for which Daukes seems likely to have been the architect.

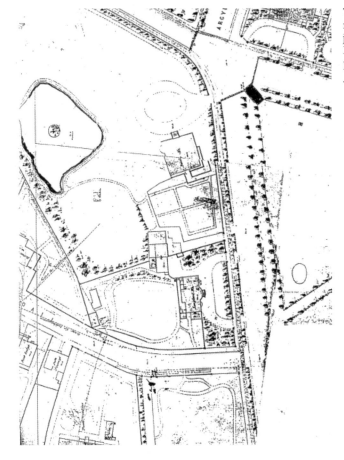

The existence of The Park spa; clearly marked as a black rectangle; at the junction with Park Place and Argyle Place; now Grafton road; dates this plan as in the 1850s

THE PARK SPA.

A Spring producing an abundant supply of Pure Saline Water having been recently found to exist on the Park Estate, at a depth of about 50 feet, possessing all the properties of the old well-known No. 4 of the established Spas, Mr. BILLINGS, the Proprietor, has tested its efficacy by obtaining from Messrs. Heathfield and Burgess, of London, the analysis, which will be found in the Appendix: it proves the Water to be of somewhat greater strength than any yet found in Cheltenham.

A small classic Pump Room has recently been erected over the well sunk by Samuel Bendall, the forty years' experienced Well-sinker and Pumper of the Montpellier Spa, and under the recommendation of eminent Members of the Faculty, aided by Bendall's practical experience, the Waters have for some time been administered to the Public in their purity, and proved to be extremely efficacious.

The most influential of the Gentry in the neighbourhood having patronised the Spa, Bendall has become the Lessee, and issued the following moderate scale of charges for drinking the Waters.

Terms of Subscription.

	£.	s.	d.
A Family for the Season	1	1	0
Two Persons of the same Family	0	15	0
Single Subscription, ditto	0	10	6
Ditto for one Month	0	5	0

The above Subscription includes the privilege of using the Park Promenades and Drives nearly two miles in extent, which afford to the Invalid and Valetudinarian a cool and delightful Promenade during the heat of Summer.

Non-Subscribers to the Spa using the Walks and Drives are subject to the following payments to the Proprietor towards the annual expense of keeping them in repair, and Subscription Books are open at the Spa for that purpose..

	£.	s.	d.
For the Drives and Walks	0	10	6
" Walks only	0	5	0
" Using a Wheel Chair	0	7	6

A further feature of the lake is the present Boathouse marked on the 1884 OS map, its charming design deserving designation as a Listed building.

1999 Demolition of Fullwood hostel.

Of the subsequent development of The Park, Fullwood had various owners: Mrs MacKnight Crawford added the west-facing solarium in 1899, now shorn of its projecting gables, but retaining her initials in the centre pediment glass. By 1912 the Ursuline Ladies College was in occupancy and in 1931 St Mary's Training College. Fulwood (Broadlands) had several military owners before passing to St Mary's College and ultimately to the College of Higher Education now the University of Gloucestershire.

Elwes Building

The development of the area as an academic campus was associated with the expansion of the institutions taking over some of the villas both within The Park and also those situated on the periphery, as well as adding purpose-built provision for teaching, library and hostel accommodation. Nevertheless the original concept of 1835 survives in its axis of the Elephant Walk, in the Arcadian woodland, in the lake and the grand houses of Fullwood and Broadlands. To walk round the perimeter road, viewing even from the outside, such a landscape presents an impressive example of the 19th century vision of "rus in urbe". Little wonder those early guidebooks would describe it as being "laid out with taste and judgement".

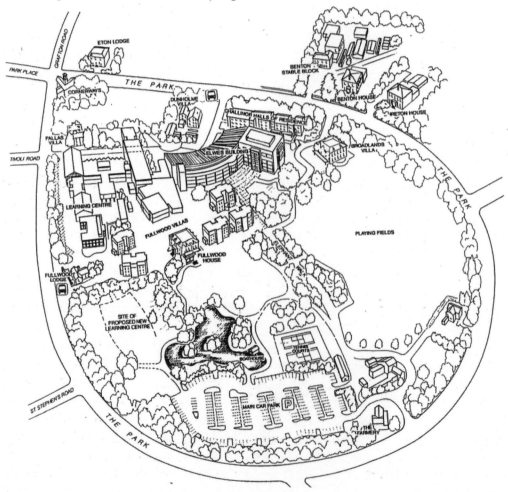

The Park Campus in the final years of the 21st century showing peripheral villas owned by The College of Higher Education.

THE PLANTING

ANY ACCOUNT OF the development of The Park must include consideration of its foliage, if only because the nineteenth century was an era of plant collecting. The emergence of the eighteenth century country house set in its landscape picturesquely enriched by trees served as an exemplar for the town park, with its winding romantic paths, thick shrubberies, and above all exotic trees.

Here Merrett's map of 1834 shows The Park in its infant state: the perimeter road, labelled Rides and Walks, is bordered by trees on both sides, while the formal drive on an axis with Moorend Park Road is complemented by serpentine paths from the northeast 'pleasure garden' and another linking the conjectural house to the lake.

But it is not until the 1855 town map that the sparse planting is replaced by a richer treatment: around the lake's winding paths, each side of the Grand Promenade, and bordering the inner perimeter. The chosen species would have included examples of the Victorian 'conifer craze' like the wellingtonia, cedar, pine and yew, as well as many of the 18th century introductions such as cypress, acacia and sweet chestnut.

The roads and footpaths themselves were now a growing problem to A.T Billings who had inherited responsibility from Thomas: in 1872 he asserted in a report to the residents of The Park Estate that for £765 the sewers were to be linked to a main public sewer instead of emptying into the Hatherley Brook; that junctions and gratings would be installed; and that he would resurface the original Leckhampton stone with Bristol,

Wickwar or other stone that has "undergone igneous action". However, blame for the roads' condition was levied at the residents "who ought to bestir themselves" and "cut down unnecessary trees and useless shrubs"! It should also be added that blocked drains and sewers were to cause in 1881 an outbreak of typhoid, which resulted in the installation of corporation-water piping.

The 1887 map reveals The Park's landscape maturity, now showing that the inner perimeter trees have been replaced by a screen of lime, sycamore and beech within the south boundary. What it does not indicate is the extent of ground cover in the form of shrubs so popular with the Victorians. For this was the age of the exotic collectors like the Chipping Campden traveller Ernest 'Chinese' Wilson.

In 1991 a selective listing of The Park's trees and shrubs showed the wide range still present: the following tables and map record their location, though the shrubs are represented by a more extensive 'pruning' for the areas lettered, with repetition of names avoided.

The very extensiveness of the planting and the passing of the years meant that a thorough assessment was required as regards both condition and visual value. Much growth of the shrubs needed thinning, while the trees dating back to the original layout were to be preserved if possible. Accordingly in 2002 an arboricultural survey was carried out concentrating on the area around the lake, and a further examination took place in 2005. In broad terms the recommendations in respect of the 143 specimens assessed, 66 were considered of value according to the criteria of condition, relationships to The Park landscape, age, form and texture, actual and expected size, and last but not least hospitality for wildlife. However 60 failed to satisfy the requirements in one or more aspects and they were regarded as meriting felling.

In 2006 consequently a thorough programme of action was carried out, not only in respect of trees but also widespread clearance of ground cover. The result was to open up views and afford space particularly around the lake and Elephant Walk.

Fortunately many of the specimens which had been part of the original layout were retained and their majestic size continued to make a significant contribution to The Park's environment. With new planting and informed management the landscape value will continue to attract, even if not to the height of effusion as reported in 1840 by the *Looker On*:

"the Zoological and Botanical Gardens have rejoiced in the recent fertilizing weather to an extent almost incredible, the foliage of the young plantations now displaying the richest varieties of tints and every foot of ground being redolent of the sweet perfume of a thousand flowers" (30 May)

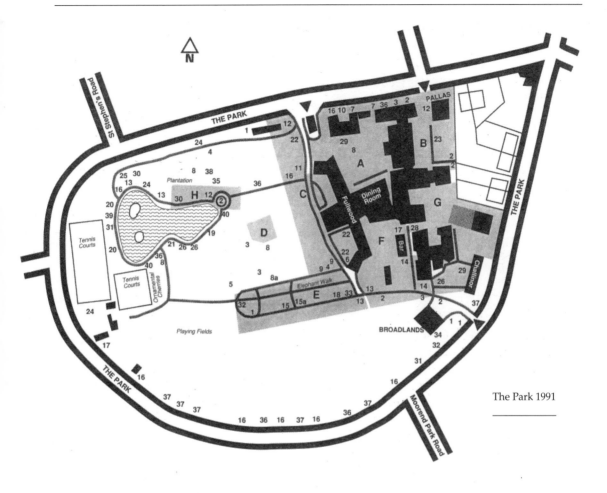

The Park 1991

TREES

Evergreen Conifers

1 Common Yew – Taxus baccata

2 Wellingtonia or Great Sequoia – Sequoiadendron giganteum

3 Deodar – Cedrus deodora

4 Brewer Spruce – Picea brewiana

5 Colorado Blue Spruce – Picea pungens var, glauca

6   Western Red Cedar – Thuja plicata

7   Monterey Cypress – Cupressus macrocarpa

8   Glaucus Atlas Cedar – Cedras atlantica var, glauca

8a Incense Cedar – Calocedrus decurrens

9   Italian Cypress – Cupressus sempervirens

10 Norway Spruce – Picea abies

11 Lawsion Cypress – Chamaecyparis lawsoniana

12 Nootka Cypress – Chamaecyparis nootkatensis

13 Austrian Pine – Pinus nigra var, nigra

13a Bhutan Pine – Pinus walichiana

Italian Cypress cone

Broad Leaf Trees

14 Laurel Magnolia – Magnolia grandiflora

15 Tulip Tree – Liriodendron tulipifera

15a Tree of Heaven – Ailanthus altissima

16 Common Beech – Fagus sylvatica

17 Copper Beech – Fagus sylvatica 'Purpurea'

18 Cut-Leaf Beech – Fagus sylvatica 'Heterophylla'

19 Goat Willow – Salix caprea

20 Hornbeam – Carpinus betulis

21 Bird Cherry (garden form) – Prunus padus 'Commutata'

22 Purple Leaved Plum – Prunus cerasifera 'Pissardii'

23 Weeping Ash – Fraxinus excelsior 'Pendula'

24 Horse Chestnut – Aesculus hippocastanum

25 Red Horse Chestnut (garden form) – Aesculus x carnea 'Briotii'

26 Himalayan Birch – Betula utilis

27 Young's Weeping Birch – Betula pendula 'Youngii'

28 Norway Maple 'Crimson King'- Acer platanoides 'Crimson king'

29 Japanese Cherry 'Amanogawa' – Prunus cultivar

30 Holm Oak – Querus ilex

31 Common Oak – Querus robur

32 False Acacia or Locust Tree – Robinia pseudoacacia

Common Beech

Horse Chestnut

33   London Plane – Platanus x acerifolia

34   Walnut – Juglans nigra

35   Corkscrew Willow – Salix matsudana 'Tortuosa'

36   Sycamore – Acer pseudoplatanus

37   Common Lime – Tilia x europaea

38   White Poplar – Polulus alba

39   Sweet Chestnut – Castanea sativa

40   Common Ash – Fraxinus excelsior

41   Rowan or Mountain Ash – Sorbus aucuparia

Deciduous Conifers

42   European Larch – Larix decidua

43   Swamp or Bald Cypress – Taxodium distichum

Sycamore

SHRUBS

A   Arburus, Ceanothus, Jasmine, Garrya

B   Pyracantha, Cotoneaster

C   Magnolia, Spirea, Choisya, Ilex, Mahonia

D   Phlomis, Yucca

E   Abelia, Acer, Amelanchier, Aucuba, Buddleia, Cornus, Continus, Escallonia, Euonymus, Ficus, Hamamelis, Ilex, Laburnum, Laurus, Philadelphus, Prunus, Viburnum

F   Fuschia

G   Arbutus, Berberis, Deutzia, Hydrangea, Skimmia, Ribes, Symphoricarpus, Tamarix, Weigela, Wisteria

H   Hypericum, Pieris, Thuja, Juniperis

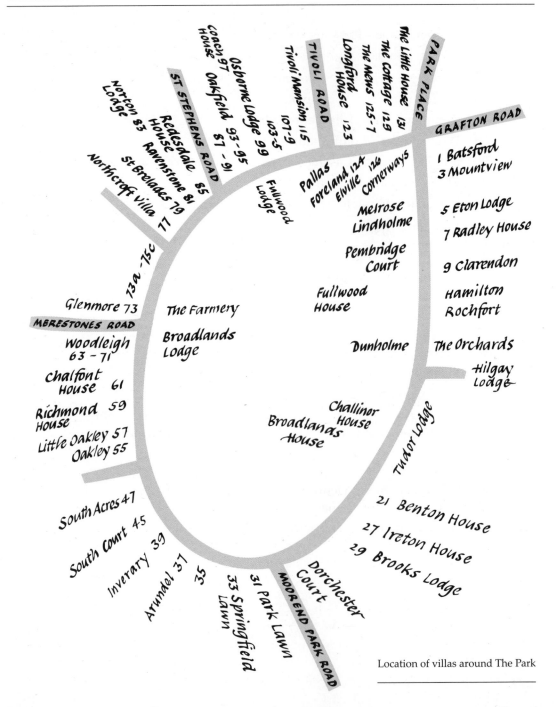

Location of villas around The Park

THE VILLAS

I F MERRETT'S MAP of 1834 provides an indication of what was intended, there can be little doubt that The Park would have been circled by detached villas each occupying its plot of one-third acre, and a road lined with trees. Whether the architectural style would have been as repetitive as Merrett suggests, or whether the example of Pittville, with its alternating terraces and individual houses, might have been adopted is open to question. Perhaps the evidence of three semi-detached pairs, all amongst the early building, represents a tentative acknowledgement. However there is also here a lack of emphasis by special treatment at the junctions with the feeder roads. Furthermore, it is not possible to know what the facades of these proposed villas were to be.

In the event, progress in actual building was slow and spasmodic. As might be expected, the plots nearest Park Place were the first to be developed; the original numbering of the properties beginning there and going anti-clockwise, the location of no. 1 Park Villas being that of the present 26 Park Place. A survey of the known dates of building in The Park reveals that by 1835 there were two, only one being occupied; by 1855 there were twenty-six though clearly others fall into broader time categories with 1835 to 1850 representing the greatest expansion. It must be noted that losses have also occurred: Boteler/Fernihurst, Tudor Lodge, and Woodlands being notable examples. There have been additions, too, either as substitution or infill, and here a question has to be raised as to what is the appropriate style: scholarly copy, contemporary version or 'modern'?

Chronologically all the building in The Park may be designated late Regency, Victorian, Edwardian or modern, since there is none earlier than 1830. However, stylistically, there are subdivisions reflecting fashions and influences. Those do not necessarily conform to the above-mentioned periods or indeed follow consecutively; they may display purity or prove a mix of style; there may be anachronisms or inventive interpretation. But broadly, the scale and materials employed respect the ambience of this environment and this range of idiom can be observed in miniature by the gate piers which are such a valuable feature of the street scene, their designs ranging through all manner of classical treatment. It is hardly surprising therefore that twenty-four of these villas have been included in the List of Buildings of Architectural or Historical interest.

The Georgian period was 1720-1821 but The Park represents only the last years of pure Georgian in houses displaying the characteristics of simplicity and regularity of windows and doorways, the former having twelve panes arranged as a double square, the latter beneath a fanlight and enriched by a porch supported by classical columns; there are three floors separated visually on the façade by horizontal stringcourses, held in by corner pilasters, and surmounted by a parapet behind which is a range of dormer windows in the roof.

The use of stucco imitating stone is a precursor to the Regency period 1820-30 which retains many Georgian features but adapts and introduces fresh idioms. Now the parapet is succeeded by generous eaves, the glazing bars of windows become thinner and there is a general lightness in the whole façade. This playfulness finds expression in the introduction of pointed arches in the glazing and a preference sometimes for less symmetry of doorway and window. The emphasis is on width rather than height, often including a bow at the side. A particular feature employed in Cheltenham is the shallow recessed arch over ground floor windows, which may be divided into a centre sash with flanking panes.

It is worth emphasising that Georgian and Regency are styles which have very blurred demarcation; moreover their architectural identities do not correspond time-wise with the regnal years. And what is so for those periods is even more true for the following Victorian. Much Early–Victorian draws on the tradition of Regency while, throughout the remainder of the 19th century, style becomes a matter of 'pick-&-mix'. The villas may have echoes of Queen Anne, that is pre-Georgian, in their pronounced eave brackets, or their conspicuous corner quoins; their window proportions may exaggerate or be framed by elaborate plasterwork; their bay windows echo Gothic, or their bargeboards the Tyrolean. On the other hand there may be careful copying of classical, or a desire to capture Italian flavour with balcony, tower or balustrade. Some may even wish to emulate Paxton's glasshouses with a conservatory! Small wonder, the Victorian – and Edwardian – period has been dubbed the "battle of the styles".

And in a sense that 'battle' continues today for The Park has new building which represents on the one hand 'tradition' with copies of the past, and on the other 're-interpretation': Clarendon has provided the model for Radley, Firleaze, Hamilton & Rochfort; 37 Arundel for 45, Southcourt. The villas on the west side owe very little, except scale, to predecessors. Their thin detailing and self – conscious turrets are but brief acknowledgement to the villa concept.

The variety of the villas' architectural features is echoed by their range of uses: from private house, hotel, school, nursing home, spiritualist church, design offices, to government departments. And this can be further reflected in the ownership: gas board, commercial firm, educational establishment, or religious order. Then there is the range of occupiers: military and naval officers, medics, academics, clerics, magistrates, and solicitors. All can be found in their individual histories which follow.

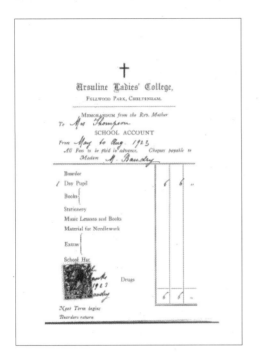

1930s advertisement

Perhaps the following extract from the deeds of 1835 for Arundel best conveys The Park's aspiration:

"To preserve gentility, access [is permissible] either on foot or on horseback, with or without light carriages of every description, but not with carts, wagons, or other heavy vehicles except such as may be necessary for conveying coal and other necessaries… No building in the front garden [is allowed], which must be kept as an ornamental pleasure ground…. The piers, gates, railings and garden walls…[and] … the elevation must stay as now for ever hereafter…enlargements of the house [may be] allowed if the front is covered with roman cement or stone…no washing is to be hung out at front…no trade… no searching for or selling of mineral waters… no making of bricks or tiles….no burning of lime."

INNER CIRCLE

(a) *(SL)* **2, CORNERWAYS** (1933) GONIA (1887) = corner (Greek), FLORENCE GROVE (1882), FLORENCE VILLA (1871) after one of Billings's daughters

(b) 1861   E. FRAMPTON (land) to R. READ and S. DAUKES; also W. SMITH (land) to W. ROBINSON

(c) 1863   S.B. BILLINGS, solicitor. Villa and spa and pleasure ground.
      1865   built
      1870   Mrs MCNAIR
      1872   S.B. BILLINGS
      1874   H. MALKIN to G.C. PIMBURY
      1882   Miss M.J. TAYLOR
      1906   Mrs E. WHITE to W. BELL-HAWORTH MA 1927
      1933   Dr H.T. PALMER
      1938   Dr A.J. BROUGHTON-EDGE MB
      1953   T.D. SEARLE, F.P. TREASURE
      1968   Mrs N.L. TREASURE
             ST. MARY'S TRAINING COLLEGE

(d) T-shape plan with two storeys gabled on the north. Attic to the west. A four storey tower-porch with pairs of round arch and cross-light openings. Sloping buttresses. Wide bracketed eaves.

(e) On the site of Park Spa instigated by Billings appropriating the Grecian lodge from Park Place; served as an estate office for Billings.

(g) G.C.W. PIMBURY born 1867, son of G.C. PIMBURY, played rugby for County Durham and Harlequins

W.B. HAWORTH schoolmaster Cheltenham College 1887-1925, churchwarden S. STEPHENS

(a) *(LL)* **6, MELROSE**, MELROSE VILLA (1876), MELROSE PRIVATE HOTEL (1930)

(b) Mid nineteenth century

(c) 1876   General MCCAUSLAND CB
    1887   Mrs PARSONS
    1902   W.R. PORCHER, Misses PARKIN
    1921   Miss M. PARKIN
    1927   Melrose House Private Hotel: Mrs H.M. COBBOLD
    1930   Miss F.L. BOTTENS proprietor
    1937   Homeland Estate Agency W.S.P. MILES
    1939   Mrs BENNETT; Lieutenant Colonel K.D.F. MCCASKILL OBE;
            A.S. CRUIKSHANK; L. CLIFT
    1942   Mrs BENNETT; K. WORMALD; A.S. CRUIKSHANK
    1950   F. MAXLOW
    1957   F. MAXLOW, Mrs JOHNSON, W. DEMBOWSKI
    1960   Squadron Leader J.P. THRUSH, Mrs JOHNSON, W. DEMBOWSKI
    1963   D. KEMP, Miss M.E. ASTON, Miss G.M. SHADWELL, Mrs V.V. ATTWOOD
    1968   F.E. JAMES, Miss M.E. ASTON, Mrs L.J. MARSHALL
    1970   F.E. JAMES, Miss M.E. ASTON, Mrs L.J. MARSHALL, R.C. ROSLIN-LAMBERT
    1973   J.R. GRIFFIN, DAVIS, D.N. FISHER, G.K. SHIMMIN, Ms J.L. HARRIS
    1999*   5 flats

(d) Large semi-detached pair with no 8. Stucco. Three storeys and a basement. The windows are grouped in threes, the centre one in the top floor has a pointed arch gable, slight breakforward at centre. Porch at side arch entrance and side. Bracketed eaves.

(g) PORCHER schoolmaster at Cheltenham College, 1863-98

MCCAUSLAND East India Company, Lieutenant General 29th Regiment of Native Infantry, CB for service during the Indian Mutiny

(a) *(LL)* **8, LINDHOME**

(b) Mid nineteenth century

(c) 1870   Major General GRAHAM
    1887   Mrs MACPHERSON and Mrs LUARD
    1902   Lieutenant Colonel W. MOLLAN CB
    1916   General C.A. MOORE
    1927   Misses YEADON-JONES also bought part of the orchard opposite 1933
    1950   H.C. and W.L. KING
    1957   H.C. KING
    1963   M. OPARENKO, C.L. WILSON, S.C. STEPHENSON, E. MILLER
    1968   M. OPARENKO, A.B.D. TIFFEN, S.C. STEPHENSON, M.C. STORR

1971 M. OPARENKO, G.L. DAVIES, S.C. STEPHENSON, M.C. STORR
1973 B. BULLINGHAM, ROSLIN-LAMBERT, J. CATRIS, D. RAY
1999* Ms M. GANT, J. ISOM, Ms P. KINNEAR

(d) As for no 6, except the top floor only has a single window under the arch gable.

(g) MOLLAN took an army role in the Indian Mutiny 1857-9

W.L. KING MC, TD, MA produced reprint of Gloucestershire and Bristol atlas (1777)

(a) **10, PEMBRIDGE COURT**

(b) 1866

(c) 1887 T.A. VIGNE
1916 Colonel C. VULLIAMY
1921 Mrs VULLIAMY
1933 F. APPS
1939 Lieutenant Colonel A. NORTHEN CBE DSC
1950 E. FOX-HAWKES
1957 E.V. RIDGE

(d) The façade mirrors that of Dunholme with minor variations in the window pattern.

(g) APPS was India (army?)

(a) **KINELLAN** north part of PEMBRIDGE

(b) As for PEMBRIDGE

(c) 1936 Lieutenant Colonel F.M. CLOSE OBE
1957 F. CLOSE, Lieutenant Colonel J.S. CLOSE OBE
1973 D.A. RUSCA

(a) *(LL)* **12, DUNHOLME**, COVALS (1887)

(b) 1866 W.M. SMITH, builder

(c) 1870 R.T. PORTER
1887 W. HENDERSON
1891 Miss DAWKINS
1904 Deputy Surgeon General J. LANDALE
1921 Mrs LANDALE
1927 E. TRENOUTH
1930 Mrs DWYER private hotel

1939   The Park Nursing Home
1946   St. Mary's Training College

(d) Three storeys. Stucco over brick. Corner Quoins. Central arched entrance; window arrangement that mirrors that of neighbouring Pembridge Court.

(a) **ELWES BUILDING**
     H. ELWES Lord-Lieutenant of Gloucestershire

(b) 1994

(c) Concave to east. A three storey combination of student union hall with teaching provision and hall, lecture theatre. The centre divider serves as reception area to full height. Exterior cladded panels.

(a) *(SL)* **22, BROADLANDS HOUSE,** gates and piers and those looking along Moorend Park Road, FULWOOD HOUSE (1895)

Broadlands formerly
Fulwood House in 1885

(b) 1854   site bought from A. TAYLOR by J.M. GILBERTSON to build.

(c) 1870   Canon GRIFFITHS
     1873   A. CATHCART
     1885   General J.P. MARTIN
     1890   J.G.K. YOUNG to General C.B. FULLER RRA
     1898   Surgeon Major I. NEWTON IMS
     1930   Mrs NEWTON
     Second World War - Ministry of Labour
     1941   St. Mary's Training College

(d) Two storeys. Hipped roof on the south east, gabled on north west. Doric pilasters at the north east entrance. Wide brackets under eaves. Windows on the rear with blind-boxes and louvred shutters. Conservatory removed on the south west wall, 1990s.

(e) 1941 bought by St. Mary's Training College and requisitioned temporarily by Ministry of Labour.

(f) 1885 on east side "tennis lawn well-sheltered by shrubbery…south side fine level paddock with cowshed and enclosed yard sheltered from the road by a wide belt of trees and shrubs". Pair of gate piers to entrance; also another pair facing Moorend Park Road, marking former avenue of 1843.

(g) NEWTON Churchwarden SS. Philip and James church

GRIFFITHS former Vice-Dean of Rochester Cathedral

(a) *(SL)* **FULLWOOD PARK**

(b) 1847

(c) 1870 E.S. POTTER
1887 A. LITTLEDALE
1899 T. MACKNIGHT-CRAWFORD (L. M-C. widow by then?)
1912 URSULINE LADIES COLLEGE £4,500 St. Angela's High School for Girls
1929 Closure of Home and Colonial College, 30 places offered to St. Mary's College £1,200 but hostel foundation stone not laid till 1939 (31 March)
1931 St. Mary's Training College plus 12 acres including 12 grass and 2 hard tennis courts £7,500
1939 Hostel wings. Evacuation to Llandrindod Wells, Wales
Dec 1940 College returned

Ironwork on main door

(d) Two Storeys and attic. Flattened hip roof. Centre door solid porch, Doric pilasters, studded door. West veranda wood with chinoise lattice, pediment 'MC' glass c.1900, truncated length, further solarium on east 2000.

Solarium

(e) 1912 School
1932 St. Mary's Training College

(f) For history of development of grounds see full account above.

(L) boathouse pre-1887, timber octagonal dovecote, weathervane.

North entrance quadrant, piers with copper monograms (as in pediment of single-storey Lodge), railings with spearhead and circle motifs.

Hostel wings 1939, Fullwod Villas 1999.

The Ursuline Order Convent Ladies College between 1913 and 1931

(a) FULLWOOD LODGE

(b) 1839 architect S.W. DAUKES

(c) 1847 A. TAYLOR
H. PERKINS

(d) Italianate. Two storeys. On the west side of the north entrance to The Park. Demolished 1870s

(a) FULLWOOD COTTAGE

(b) unknown

(c) 1937 H.J. WAINE

(d) Location may have been at the west end of the Elephant Walk as suggested on post-1897 map

(a) *(LL)* **FULLWOOD LODGE**

(b) Late nineteenth century

(c) 1937   G. BOND

(d) Single storey. The North entrance is the centre of the entrance to The Park

Central pediment bears carved monogram replicating those on gate piers

Carving on pediment

(a) **THE FARMERY**, PRIEST'S COTTAGE (1930), FARM LODGE (1927)

(b) Early twentieth century

(c) 1927   F.C. BRIDGMAN, gardener to URSULINE LADIES COLLEGE
1937   F. TOWNSEND, butcher
1973   F.E. SLADE

(d) Detached Two storeys. Brick

(a) **BROADLANDS LODGE**

(b) Early twentieth century

(c) 1927   E.J. INGLES, gardener to BROADLANDS

(d) Detached Two storeys. Brick

(a) *(SL)* **PALLAS VILLA** (1921), EASTON GREY (1911)

(b) 1833-50

(c) 1874   E. ARMITAGE to G.G. PAINE
1876   Mrs W.S. BIRCH
1899   G.G. PAINE to Mrs E. O'CONNERSMITH
1903   Mrs E. GROWSE
1912   URSULINE LADIES COLLEGE, Mrs E.O. GROWSE
1927   A.J. IRWIN
1933   W.F. DUDLEY
1939   CHELTENHAM LADIES COLLEGE
1941   Mrs HENSMAN
1946   St. Mary's Training College

(d) Two storeys and attic. Stucco over brick. Centre door, pilastered conservatory

(e) 1912 school and 1939 school boarding house

1946 purchase as college made possible by legacy of Emily L. Brooks, student 1896-8, lecturer 1918-36, life governor 1938-46. She also bequeathed books and pictures and financial help in landscaping grounds.

(a) **LYNCOURT**

(b) 1830-50

(c) 1870   Miss UNDERHILL
    1911   Miss BOOTH
    1916   Miss BOND
    1921   URSULINE LADIES COLLEGE

(d) Detached villa, Stucco. Linked to Belfont. Demolished circa 1960

(a) **BELFONT**

(b) 1830-50

(c) 1871   Lieutenant General R. BUDD
    1887   Misses BUDD
    1891   W. WILLCOCKS
    1911   A. BOND
    1922   URSULINE LADIES COLLEGE

(d) Detached villa. Mirror of Pallas Villa. Demolished 1960

(g) BUDD Madras Army from 1812 to 1874, died 1885

(a) **124, FORELAND**

(b) 1897

(c) 1902   Captain SHAKESPEAR RN
     1911   S.A. PYM
     1916   H.J. LAWRIE
     1920   W.H. LYALL MBE, Mrs F.E. ABERNETHY
     1927   G.T.H. BRACKEN
     1928   Mrs COLLIER
     1939   Miss A. BLAKENEY
     1945   Major A.P. POE
     1957   Captain A. POE DSC RN
     1958   Dr. A.B.S. MULES
     1981   K. TODD

(d) Pair of semi-detached villas with 126. Two storeys. Bargeboards design is Tyrolean and is identical with No. 1 Ashford Road

(g) LYALL b. 1875, son of D. Lyall MC Deputy Inspector-General of hospitals and Fleets.

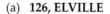

(a) **126, ELVILLE**

(b) 1897

(c) 1902   Mrs E. GROWSE
     1911   A.G. WHITBY
     1930   Mrs A.B. WHITBY
     1957   A.B. WHITBY
     1999*   P. CADOGAN

(d) As for no. 124

(g) A.B. WHITBY, born 1899 son of A.G. Whitby, Civil Engineer Shar States and in Burma.

OUTER CIRCLE

(a) *(SL)* **1, BATSFORD HOUSE**, 2 PARK PROMENADE (1835)

(b) 1830-50

(c) 1840   I.D. LUARD
     1873   Major VIALLS
     1878   G.P. MASON
     1887   Colonel BLAIR
     1902   Mrs C. HUTCHINSON, MISS CLOSE
     1916   Mrs CAVE-BROWN-CAVE
     1927   Colonel E.C. DOWSE
     1933   Brigadier General G.D. CLOSE CB
     1936   Mrs C.E. DOWSE
     1961   Miss E.M. BRAMWELL, G.T. MULLALLY
     1963   Miss E.M. BRAMWELL, G.T. MULLALLY, Major C.F. COX MBE
     1968   Miss E.M. BRAMWELL, G.T. MULLALLY, L.C.W. CROWTHER
     1999*   J. HINTON (1) C. JENNINGS (2) J. GODSON (3)

(d) Semi-detached with no. 3, Mountview. Two storeys. The porches are set in an angle:
     the left is raised and extended to full height and the right projects at ground floor level.
     The windows have architraves and on ground floor cornices on brackets. The left house
     porch has an added entrance. Round arch staircase sashes. Wide eaves

(g) DOWSE, son of R.R. Dowse, surgeon, after Sandhurst and 45th Foot Regiment took part
     in Tirch Expedition 1897/8

(a) *(SL)* **3, MOUNTVIEW**, BALLYRAINE (1927), GLENGAR (1921),
     1 PARK PROMENADE (1835)

(b) 1830-50

(c) 1838   W.F. HEATHER
     1840   Mrs NICHOLS
     1851** Mrs KEMP, three children and two servants
     1873   G.P. MASON
     1876   F.W. JAMES
     1891   Mrs LLOYD

1912	Miss M.E. ALLEN
1916	Miss HERBERT, Miss ALLEN
1920	H.L. MEADOWS
1933	Mrs O.M. MEADOWS
1950	Mrs A. CAREY
1957	L.S. HILLS
1973	L.F. GAYLARD
1999*	five flats

- (d) See no. 1 description

(f) In 1951 the coach house fronting Grafton Lane was converted to a dwelling known as the Old Coach House. A pair of gate piers with panelled shaft, frieze, cornice and pyramidal cap

---

(a) **OLD COACH HOUSE** (Grafton Lane, east of Mountview)

(b) As for Mountview

(c)

1890	I. BEAR, Ms M.L. HOWARD,
	J.A. COPLAND to Mrs C. CORMOULS, Ms A. BEAR
1912	Ms C. CORMOULS LEGG to C.M. HAWARD
	C.M. HAWARD to Ms M.E. ALLEN
1951	Mrs A. CAREY to T.V. HOW, builder for conversion
1961	Mrs E.M. SELBIE
1963	H.L. VINCENT
1995	C.E. JONES, R. MALPASS for £100,000
2007	Miss A. PYKE

(d) Two storey with a north extension. Stucco over brick. Hipped roof. The entrance is via an extension

(g) VINCENT at GCHQ, amateur wind player

JONES retired NHS manager in psychiatry; MALPASS designer House of Fraser (see Mitford Lodge, Tivoli Road)

(a) *(SL)* **5, ETON LODGE**, ETON LODGE HOTEL (1942), ETON VILLA (1860)

(b) 1846   WILLIAM J. POPE to Charles Twining builder

(c) 1851**   H.P. WHATELY and one son, six daughters and one gardener
     1853   Misses WHEATLY or WHATELY
     1860   Miss M. RIDLER
     1870   Mrs CAMERON
     1871   Mrs W. ROBINSON
     1873   Lieutenant Colonel G.E. WATSON
     1880   Surgeon General N. HEFFERNAN
     1902   R.W. HARVEY
     1911   Mrs HEFFERNAN, Mrs F. STEWART
     1920   A.F.R. CONDER MC MD
     1942   Eton Lodge Hotel
     1956   W. BECK, Miss PHILLIPS, Mrs J.M. WHITE, J. LOWLEY, Mrs GREENSLADE
     1961   W. BECK, Miss PHILLIPS, Miss KIRKLAND, J. LOWLEY, Mrs GREENSLADE
     1963   W. BECK, Miss PHILLIPS, Miss KIRKLAND, W.A. KING, Mrs GREENSLADE
     1966   St. Mary's Training College
     2000   Sold for Residential use

(d) Two storey. End rusticated pilasters. Windows moulded architraves, ground floor have cornices on modillions. Central doorcase Doric pilasters, frieze and cornice with flattened pediment

(g) CONDER son of C.R. Conder, born 1848 Cheltenham, army officer, explorer of Palestine, died 1910 at St Oswalds Tivoli Road.

(a) **RADLEY** on site of FRIARSWOOD

(b) 1999

(c) 1961   T.V. BROWN (FRIARSWOOD)

(d) Semi-detached villas. Stucco over brick. Side entrances. Balcony scrolled ironwork.

     Two storeys, basement and attic

(a) *(SL)* **9, CLARENDON**, possible association with Edward Hyde, Earl of Clarendon, ELLESMERE LODGE till 1962

(b) 1834-8

(c) 1835   Conveyance "except all mines and minerals and all medicinal waters." Thomas Billings to FREEMAN PADMORE

    1838   J. HART
    1840   Mrs FEATHERSTONE
    1847   Miss C. ENGLAND
    1850   Mrs ENGLAND
    1855   J. WILSON
    1870   Captain J. MAYNE
    1871   Major E.W. AGAR
    1878   J.F. SEVIER
    1891   Miss H.T. JOHNSON
    1933   Mrs REVOIRA
    1962   Mrs KRIER
    1968   G. SIDDONS-WHITE dentist £4,000
    1973   Sarah Marie HYDE to C.D. CARPENTER
    1982   G. WAREING
    1994   R. CANNON
    1995   J.M. JAMES, Ms J. MAJOLINO-LENOIR (Garden flat)

(d) Two storeys and basement. Doric pilasters and fluted Ionic pilasters to central breakforward. Windows have architraves and first floor have sills and cornices on console brackets, the centre one is pedimented. Railings to centre steps have scrolled rods; Entrance porch has architrave with wreathes. Parapet with concealed roof behind

(f) Period summerhouse, ¼ acre plot

(g) E. AGAR, son of Major E.W. Agar, distinguished Army career, C.M.G

JOHNSON bought part of adjoining orchard 1926

(a) **HAMILTON HOUSE** and **ROCHFORT HOUSE** on site of MOSELLA HOUSE and former orchard

(b) 1999

(d) Semi-detached pair. Two storeys. Entrances at sides north and south. Style based on Clarendon. Concealed roof

(a) **MOSELLA** from Luxembourg village on bank of Moselle

(b) 1955   architect SMITHSON of Rainger Rogers and Smithson; builder SURMAN

(c) 1955   J. KRIER
    1971   M. KRIER
    1980   let to visiting American lecturers on exchange programme with St. Marys Training College
    1999   demolished

(d) Neo-georgian symmetrical façade of two storeys, with centre entrance. Rendered with coarse white sand from Loch Morar; roof slates from Delabole Quarry, Cornwall

(g) KRIER owner of Maison Kunz patisserie in Promenade.

(h) 1980 corroded gas pipe caused explosion and fire as no shut-off valve to road. Two firemen injured. Event led to regulation that external stop-cock or exposed pipe be obligatory

---

(a) **THE ORCHARDS** in former orchard

(b) Early twentieth century. Two storeys. Rendered. L-Shaped

(c) 1927   R. SAYNOR THOMPSON
    1936   V.W. PERCIVAL, dental surgeon
    1957   Mrs B.G. PERCIVAL MBE
    1968   R.F. WALKER
    1970   Mrs D.C. WEST
    1973   G.W. WEST
    1974   A.R. MACINDOE
    1979   B.W. KING
    2009   Demolished
    2010   M. PHILLIPS

(a) *(SL)* **HILGAY LODGE (**1916), TWICKENHAM VILLA (1855), TWICKENHAM PIKE (1851)

(b) 1834-40

(c) 1847   W.J. POPE
    1851**   J. COCKER, retired bleacher
    1855   Captain Sir Thomas THOMPSON RN
    1856   Sale of contents
    1870   M.P. SMITH
    1878   G. CADELL
    1887   Miss FLETCHER
    1902   Mrs S.P. JANION

1916	D. MACKENZIE
1921	Colonel C.T. DUCAT, Indian Army
1930	Mrs C. DUCAT
1970s	J. CAMPBELL - E. SWINDEN
1995	Melwin Investments Ltd c/o Freeth Cartwright Upper Parliament, St. Nottingham
1999*	N. SHUBER
2006	Renovation following vandalism and fire 2005

(d) Stucco over brick. Hipped slate roof. Two tall ridge stacks. Pilasters. Tent-roof hood to entrance and south return window.

(f) Set in oval grounds with gate piers facing west and railings replacing those with circle motif removed after vandalism.

(g) W.G. DUCAT son of Colonel Ducat, born 1909, scholarship from Cheltenham College to Eton but died there 1923.

(a) **TUDOR LODGE** (1837) on site of Whitfield House

(b) 1839   S.W. DAUKES, architect

(c)

1839	S. DAUKES, Rear-Admiral O'BRIEN
1840	G. THOMSON
1847	G. TURNER
1850	Revd J.E. RIDDLE
1859	For Sale
1870	Mrs HAINES
1871	Mrs E. HARRIS
1876	RHYS GRIFFITHS
1887	R. SYKES
1891	Colonel E.W. GOLDING
1902	Mrs E. W. GOLDING
1916	T.C. KERANS / KEARNES
1930	J.C. MACKAY JP
1937	Christian Spiritualist Church; J. LILLEY
1942	The Sanctuary Nursing Home Miss SAVEALL, matron
1957	Colonel A.V. HOLDRIDGE OBE
1964	Demolished

(d) Tudor style villa. Hood moulds to windows. Ornate bargeboards to gables. Chimney stacks. Demolished 1964 replaced by a terrace of three-storey townhouses.

(f) *(SL)* Corner octagonal pier with gothic panelling at south west corner survives from original garden, and wall of stables with pointed arch openings at east also survive.

(g) S.W. DAUKES, born 1811 at Worcester. Articled to architect J. Pritchett of York; practised at Gloucester and Cheltenham by 1841; Architect to Birmingham and Gloucester Railway 1839-42; Designed churches, Cheltenham railway station, Royal Agricultural College Cirencester, Francis Close Hall, Cheltenham and Colney Hatch Asylum. Purchased the Park Estate 1839; Died 1880.

Mrs E.W. GOLDING organised Cheltenham Pageant 1908

RIDDLE minister of St. Philips has monument in St. James' Church

---

(a) **1-10 TUDOR LODGE** Terrace of 10 houses, architect J. BROOM

(c) 1972   R. STATT, FARR, M. STEADMAN, SLOAN, D.L. STEVENS, EXCELL, OLDHAM, BAKER, SHIPWAY

    1999*   R. STATT (1), H. AGG (2), W.M. CHEUNG (3), M. STEADMAN (4), J. ASPEY (5), R. PARKER (6), R. HARRIS (7), M. MURDOCH (8), M. BARTOSCH (9), K. STAIGHT (10)

(d) Terrace of 10 houses. Three storeys. Brick. The southernmost house has a conservatory addition.

(a) *(SL)* **21, BENTON HOUSE,** THE ELMS (1916), GROVE HOUSE (1851)

(b) 1838

(c) 1838   Admiral Sir R.T. RICKETTS, Bart
    1846   land J.L. MORTIMER to A.K. BAKER
    1853   K. LUMB
    1855   Lady RICKETTS, K. LUMB
    1870   R.K. LUMB
    1872   Mr SHIPLAND
    1873   W. SERGEAUNT
    1876   J. SHAPLAND/SHIPLAND
    1887   E. DAVIS
    1916   W. BOYD
    1917   Rt Revd T. DUNN
    1921   G.W. BLATHWAYT
    1940s   DOWTY Company
    1942   rented to R. FEDDEN until 1947

1942   WESTERN COUNTIES SHOP PROPERTIES
1944   St. Mary's Training College
1971   J. MATHIS
2003   LAING HOMES for residential development

(d) Two storeys plus basement and attic. Stucco. Central door with porch two pairs of Doric pilasters, architrave frieze with triglyphs and metopes. Some windows retain blind-boxes. The ground floor balconies have scroll and lozenge motif, with tent hoods; south side verandah 'heart and honeysuckle' ironwork.

(f) Stables development intended to be called BLENHEIM MEWS

(g) 1942 Sir Roy FEDDEN rented from George Dowty. Used by Fedden design team to produce 'F' Car, rear 1,000 c.c. engine, air-cooled. Black and White coach yard at St. Margaret's Road was used as a test track. Moved from Benton to Stoke Orchard in 1947 where the company went into liquidation. Fedden went to Leyland till 1949 then joined Lord Ismay at NATO. Worked on aero-engines at Bristol Aeroplane Company and set up the Cranfield Institute of Technology (now University).

"I don't know what they're doing, but they do an awful lot of it"

The first Christmas card of Roy Fedden Ltd, 1944. It was probably drawn by Gordon Wilkins (artist / author / broadcaster), who is in the rear seat of the device being driven.

(a) *(SL)* **27, IRETON HOUSE,** MALVERN HOUSE **(1878)**

(b) 1843

(c) 1845   T.A. DALE
     1855   Mrs HAY, ? W.J. POPE
     1850   E. SANDERS
     1853   Mrs SANDERS
     1855   General LIGHTFOOT
     1863   Up for sale to the Honourable P. MORETON
     1870   Colonel A. IMPEY-LOVIBOND
     1876   Captain KELLEY
     1887   Mrs H.B. KELLEY - 1921
     1930   Mrs KELLEY
     1945   St. Mary's Training College

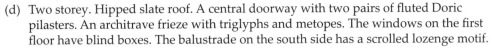

(d) Two storey. Hipped slate roof. A central doorway with two pairs of fluted Doric pilasters. An architrave frieze with triglyphs and metopes. The windows on the first floor have blind boxes. The balustrade on the south side has a scrolled lozenge motif.

(e) 1945 from domestic to educational

     2003 sold for residential development

(f) Stable development intended to be called CLARENCE MEWS

(a) *(SL)* **29, BROOKS LODGE,** BRAIDUJLE (1933) near Lisburn, Northern Ireland seat of Fulton family

(b) circa 1842

(c) 1850   Reverend G. KNIGHT
     1851** Mrs S.H. HOCKET, Ms E. TURNBULL governess
     1871   Mrs WATKINS
     1876   Mrs CHAMBERS
     1878   Surgeon General N. HEFFERNAN
     1882   General S.E. GORDON CB
     1884   Mrs GORDON
     1902   F.A. CAMERON-SMITH
     1911   Colonel P. YALDWYN
     1921   Miss LLOYD-BROWN
     1927   H. WALFORD
     1933   J.H.W. FULTON
     1942   Captain H.A. MAITLAND
     1950   A.D. HAY
     1953   R.M.E. PICK, L. SMITH garden flat

1963	R.M.E. PICK, B. COOPER garden flat
1964	A.E. WRIGHT, Lady DOWTY
1985	A. CLAMPIN
2003	J. TYRRELL

(d) Two storey. Stucco. Hipped roof. Central porch, solid porch with two pairs of Doric pilasters, architrave. Frieze and cornice. Ground floor windows elliptical recessed arches (Papworth idiom).

(f) Piers 1842 iron gates 1980

(g) GORDON brother of General Gordon of Khartoum, born 1824, died here 1883, grave at Leckhampton.

PICK was Senior History Lecturer at St. Paul's Training College.

Lady DOWTY resident post 1964, widow of Sir G. DOWTY.

TYRRELL was managing director, later vice-president, of Mitsubishi Motors UK.

(a) **ST. CLAIR:** THE PARK

(b) 1850s

(c)	
1858	V. BENJAMIN
1870	W. SCOTT
1872	Mrs W. EYTON
1873	J.J. HEBBLETHWAITE
1878	Reverend A. HALL
1887	Colonel H. DUBERLY
1891	Mrs DUBERLY
1906	H.C. CLUMB
1910	Captain J.K. LAIRD
1911	Major R. CHESTER-MASTER
1921	E.S. FLETCHER
1942	Mrs FLETCHER
1950	H.J. MEDLAND, H. HARGREAVES, J. EASTLAKE, D. WILCE
1950	A.D. HAY
1957	A. BOULTON
1963	TILLEY, baker, "crumpet-king" (owner)

(d) poor condition, 1963 demolished, 'replaced by Dorchester Court' (see Moorend Park Road)

(g) Colonel DUBERLY's wife Frances (Fanny) accompanied him to the Crimea. She witnessed action at Balaklava including the Charge of the Light Brigade and rode into Sebastopol, all these events being recorded in her diary which was published 1855 to the displeasure of Queen Victoria. In 1859 her memoir of the Indian Mutiny appeared. The Duberlys bought St Clair, Fanny surviving till 1903.

CHESTER-MASTER advocate to the High Commissioner of South Africa 1898, Commandant General South Rhodesia 1905, Chief Constable Gloucestershire 1910 was killed in the First World War. He was the brother-in-law of Arkwright, author of the hymn 'O valiant hearts'.

(a) *(SL)* **31, PARK LAWN**

(b) 1838 Builder G.G. PAINE from T. BILLINGS part of a field called WALKHAMPSTEAD

(c) 1843 T. FOTHERGILL
1851** J. ELLIOT, solicitor and Mrs PRICE
1853 Captain FENDALL
1854 Misses JEFFREY
1855 Mrs JEFFREY
1863 R. JEFFREY
1867 Lieutenant General C. GRANT
1880 M.B. JACKSON
1881 Lieutenant Colonel ALLEN
1882 Mrs BATCHELOR
1901 C.T. GARDNER CMG, Mrs J.K. LAIRD
1909 H. HOUSEHOLD
1913 Mrs WITTS
1921 Brigadier General W.J. KIRKPATRICK
1930 Brigadier General W.J. KIRKPATRICK CB
1933 Mrs KIRKPATRICK
1950 Mrs HORNBY
1961 Miss B. HORNBY, Mrs SHEATHER
1962 Miss B. HORNBY, Miss J. SCANLON SRN
1975 R. HARROD, general practitioner

(d) East half of semi-detached two storey pair with number 33, Springfield Lawn. Ashlar over brick. Concealed roof. An end entrance porch with paired pilasters, surmounted by balustrade with pierced x-motif forming balcony. Centre blind windows. Canted bay on east with veranda having slender Doric columns and balustrade 'heart and honeysuckle'

(e) 1963 Park Lawn Nursing Home: owner Mrs HORNBY was joined by Miss SCANLON and later it became student flats for St. Mary's Training College with Miss SCANLON living in self contained ground floor flat.

(f) The garden was reduced on the south by former coach house site in Moorend Park Road. Yew hedge.

(g) GARDENER was retired HM Consular Service; Mrs LAIRD, daughter of Lieutenant General C. GRANT CB, 19 Brigade RA who married the half sister of Earl Roberts of Khandahar.

(a) *(SL)* **33, SPRINGFIELD LAWN**

(b) 1838   (as for 31)

(c) 1841   G.G. PAYNE
     1843   J.C. GREEN
     1846   Miss E. SHIRCLIFFE, schoolmistress
     1854   Captain LASCELLES RN
     1867   Captain JOHNSTON
     1868   Mrs THOMPSON
     1896   Rev H.L.C. DE CANDOLE
     1900   C. TICKELL
     1911   Commander E.P. SMYTHIES RN
     1923   Colonel B.N. ANLEY
     1928   Mrs E. VAUGHAN
     1939   Colonel A.F. BAYLEY DSO
     1945   J.M.D. WINGATE
     1952   Mrs A.G. PAYTON
     1961   G.N. PATTISON
     1970   Canon E.N. DUCKER
     1977   D. STEVENS, neuro-surgeon

(d) Centre bay of façade false windows shared with attached Park Lawn (see description for 31).

(e) By 1851 it was a school for 7 pupils from India

(f) Gate piers

(g) DE CANDOLE vicar of St. James, afterwards Dean of Bristol

TICKELL bursar of Coopers Hill 1900-05

DUCKER retired here from St. Margaret's Leicester. Wrote books on psycho-analysis, and treated private patients here.

(a) *(SL)* **35, HE(A)MPSTEAD HOUSE,** (1861) GREENFIELDS after a school Mrs Evans owned in Worcestershire

(b) 1838   22 rooms G.G. PAINE

(c) 1847   T. KING, schoolmaster
1861   Mrs S. EVANS
1883   Bought at auction by Captain OSCULAPIUS FIELD
1901   Rented to Mrs WILSON
1920   I.H. HUTCHINSON and K. YULE sold to
E.E. HOLT-EVANS JP
1927   W. WEECH MA JP
1950   H.C.S. BELL
1957   Mrs SHAW
1960   Group Captain P.W. LOWE-HOLMES
1969   W. BULLINGHAM
1971   M. GEMMILL
1983   M. BOOTHMAN

(d) Two storey villa with a conservatory to the rear. Ashlar over brick. A central porch with two pairs of Doric columns, architrave, frieze with Triglyphs and metopes. Ground floor windows with elliptical arches over wide brackets to the eaves.

(e) 1841** school with 19 pupils, 5 family, governess and 9 servants

1851** school now 24 pupils, 5 family, governess and 4 servants

(f) 'Conservatory had Black Homburg vine producing 100lbs of grapes annually; stable for 3 horses' - Gemmill

2/3 acre plot

Gate piers capped

(g) 1847 owner was William Nash Skillicorne, great grandson of Henry Skillicorne. founder of Cheltenham Spa, 1st mayor of town 1876

WEECH head master Sedburgh School 1912-26, moved to 46 St. Stephens Road

GEMMILL: Technical Manager Central Electricity Generating Board

BOOTHMAN, managing director of Linotype Hell, nephew of Flight Lieutenant Boothman of Schneider Trophy contests. House was featured by Betjeman in *Daily Telegraph* 1960 as example of threatened villa when 'flats are erected on this site'.

(a) *(SL)* **37, ARUNDEL LODGE** Sussex connexion of Heather's, STONE GARTH reverted by Percival to Arundel Lodge

(b) 1835

(c) 1837   W.F. HEATHER paid £165 for plot, part of Walkhampstead Field, leased for year 1837 to S. Walters

     1851   Lady VANE

     1871   Mrs HUTCHINSON

     1881   Miss BETTS

     1891   W.F. HEATHER

     1897   H.S. MARGRETT, bought at auction £745

     1901   Ms F. FERN governess, two pupils, two servants

     1902   Mrs G.B. HODGSON

     1911   M.E. WALES

     1916   Mrs M. ATKINSON

     1930   Mrs ATKINSON, Miss RAMSFORD-COLLETT

     1942   H.G. BEARD

     1950   Mrs BEARD

     1956   Brigadier E.L. PERCIVAL DSO

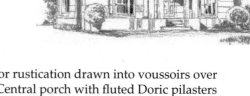

(d) Two storey. Ashlar over brick. Ground floor rustication drawn into voussoirs over segmental-arched windows. Wide eaves. Central porch with fluted Doric pilasters under entablature including triglyphs, metopes and pediment with guttae. One-storey bow on east end.

(f) Gate piers sandstone ashlar over brick, capped

(g) HEATHER, died 92 and by his will cut out *'any surviving widow'* leaving plot to G.G. Payne (first wife's nephew) who lived/owned No 35.

PERCIVAL Second World War commanded Buffs and Highland Light Infantry battalions, Recruiting Officer Gloucestershire 1956-66; (related to Lieutenant General A.E. Percival, General Officer Malaya 1941 including surrender of Singapore), died 1966.

(a) **39, INVERARY,** FIR TREES COTTAGE

(b) Mid twentieth century

(c) 1961   D.F. NEWMAN

     1963   G.F. SPARROW

     1968   Canon E.T. HUGHES

     1975   J.E. LEWIS

(d) Two storey brick villa. 1988 extended westwards. Tiled roof

(a) **45, SOUTH COURT** replacing hacienda-type house of 1960s

(b) 2006   H. PETTER of Robert Adam Associates, Winchester

(c) 1971   E. CROKER (original house)
2006   T. ROBERTS

(d) Stylistic Park Villa. Stucco. Three bays under eaves, with ground floor tripartite windows under arch recesses. Ionic four pillared porch with a shallow breakforward fanlight. First floor windows are narrow with raised surrounds. Curved screens ending with piers on each side, linking outbuildings. Interior large hall has a semi-circular apse with cantilever staircase. An octagonal sitting room with canted bay to garden. A circular dining room and lobby.

(g) CROKER Football Association Secretary

(h) 2007 Georgian Group "Giles Worsley Award" for 'new build in Georgian context'

(a) **47, SOUTHACRES,** TOSELAND (1936)

(b) 1930s

(c) 1936   T.H. PEATLING
1939   J.L. LEWIS
1950   T.L. THOMPSON
1957   Misses BULLEY, Mrs FELKIN
1999*   Mrs M. FATEH

(d) Brick single storey and basement. Central entrance. Two wings forward: the east includes a double garage, the west bedrooms. The south extends with further bedrooms. A large games room in basement.

(f) Heavy iron gates

(a) *(SL)* **55, OAKLEY**

(b) 1833-50

(c) 1847   H.W. BOOTH
1850   For sale
1855   H. CAMPS
1871   J.L. ANLEY
1916-30   Mrs A. ANLEY

      1933   H. ANLEY
      1935   M. KELLOW JP, G.M. RAINBIRD
      1936   T.H. POSTLING
      1937   M. KELLOW
      1955   E.F. LAWRENCE
      1957   R.M. MUIR, plant hire contractors
      1961   Mrs G.G. BALMER
      1968   T.L. LUND
      1975   R.C. LISSER
      1999*   M. JOYCE (55) G. ARCHER (56)
      2004   Ms A. WILSON

(d) Originally one villa now divided with Little Oakley, number 57. Two storey. Stucco over brick. Ground floor rustication. Doric porch with two pairs of fluted columns, architrave, frieze with triglyphs and metopes, cornice with guttae.

(f) gate piers with iron gates

(h) ANLEY tea planter in Ceylon

(a) **57, LITTLE OAKLEY**

(b) as for Oakley

(c)   1935   E. GWYTHER MA
      1957   Mrs D.K. MILLS
      1962   Miss F.A. PEMBER
      1972   W.G. POETON
      1973   A.T. POETON Ltd of Gloucestershire Plating Works
      1975   P.L. LYNCH
      1984   C.R. THOMPSON
      1995   A.E. ASHTON
      2007   M. JONES

(d) Originally one villa, now separate from Oakley, number 55. Two storey. Stucco over brick. Ground floor rustication. A porch of two pillars, frieze and cornice.

(f) gate piers with iron gates

(g) ASHTON architect and head of Dowty Group Property Department 1949-2004

(a) **59, RICHMOND HOUSE**

(b) 1952

(c) 1957   W.A.M. DAVIES
    1971   R.G.O. WHITE
    1977   Mrs BAILEY
    1999*   G. BAILEY

(d) Four bays. Stucco on brick. Decorative shutters

(f) pine, lopped

(a) *(SL)* **61, CHALFONT HOUSE**, WESTBOURNE LODGE (1878),
    CHALFONT LODGE (1871)

(b) 1834

(c) 1838   Captain H. BELL
    1876   W.G. COCHRANE
    1878   Revd W.H. HUTCHINSON
    1902   Mrs HUTCHINSON
    1911   Colonel H. WOODHOUSE
    1927   J.H. TUCKER
    1950   Mrs TUCKER
    1957   T.L. TALLENTIRE
    1968   R. LISSER
    1973   W.G. POETON, R. CAMKIN, J. PRITCHARD
    1999*   J. PRITCHARD
    2009   M. BLANCHFIELD

(d) Two storey. Stucco. Hipped slate roof. Central two window range projects. Single storey porch projects to the west, with a similar projection to east. Shallow Ionic porch with frieze and cornice. An east niche with tooled surround. The railings to the steps have stick balusters and a wreathed handrail.

(g) BELL, married daughter of Sir William Burdett of Claremont Lodge Montpellier; inherited estate at Woolsington, Cumberland moving there 1871, employed Middleton to design church at neighbouring Dennington; was a keen amateur archaeologist and early subscriber to Cheltenham *Looker-On* being still on its list till death 1887.

1873 advertised lease of house "3 reception, 8 bedrooms"

(a) **63, GREEN WILLOWS** (1956), WOODLEIGH (1887)

(b) 1870 Major QUENTIN
   1891 E.D. URQUHART

(c) 1911 Revd. W.H. SHAW
   1921 Lieutenant Colonel B.R.K. TARTE
   1930 H. LLOYD-DREBER
   1936 J.D. ALLISON, Mrs J.E. MIERS, Mrs A.E. DU PASQUIER
   1942 G.E.D. WHITAKER
   1957 Canon P.J. ANDREWS, Mrs A.E. DU PASQUIER, W. STANBURY
   1961 Lieutenant Colonel J. HUME DSO, F. CUMBERLAND, Mrs AIREY,
       E. TAYLOR
   1968 G. WILLIAMS
       Demolished

(h) 1876 Major QUENTIN's newly erected stables for stud of "valuable horses" destroyed by fire. Cost £600 including straw, harness. caused by sun through glass in roof? No insurance. Several people narrowly escaped when the roof collapsed.

(a) **63-71A** flats on site of GREEN WILLOWS

(b) Mid twentieth century

(c) 1971 G. WILLIAMS + BEECH LODGE, ELM LODGE, ASH LODGE, SYCAMORE LODGE, OAK LODGE

(d) Five blocks of paired three storey flats. Ground rendered. Upper floors are brick

An under ridge roof. Centre entrance for each pair

(a) **73, GLENMORE,** STARFORD HOUSE (1840) field name of west side of The Park

(b) 1830s

(c) 1840 Mrs OLDHAM
   1848 Oct: sale auction "residence of Mrs OLDHAM, OLDHAM deceased"
   1851** Mrs S. ROBERTSON, Ms C. TEA visitor, butler, coachman and four servants
   1863 advert "desirable family residence" for sale
   1870 P.W. JACKSON
   1876 J.T. COXE
   1878 Major General SHIPLEY
   1887 R. GRIFFITH
   1902 Deputy Surgeon General J.W. LANDALE
   1911 Mrs F.L. REYNOLDS-REYNOLDS

1930	C.W. CHURCHILL-BAXTER
1933	Mrs EDEN
1936	Mrs REYNOLDS-REYNOLDS
1950	E.B. TRIMMER, P. HUBBARD, T.W. HOLLAND
1957	S. FORD
	then North Gloucestershire Technical College Annexe
2006	restored to domestic use; divided into flats

(d) Villa. Stucco on brick. Three storeys plus a basement. Cornices at each floor. Centre entrance, pilasters and cornice. End pilasters

(f) 1848 "Luxuriant Pleasure Grounds, Garden, Greenhouses, Aviary and detached Stable Yard; having a frontage to the Park Drives and Promenades of 180 feet, enclosed with iron pallisading, fenced in on the southern side by a high brick wall, on the north side and at the eastern extremity by capital wood paling, the whole being belted by a thriving Plantation and Shrubbery" – auction details

(a) **73B, 73C; 75, 75A; 75B, 75C; 77A-H**

(b) 2005 on site of North Gloucestershire Technical College, later designated GlosCAT. BRYANT HOMES later PARTRIDGE developer of estate

(d) Three pairs of semi-detached villas. Stucco on brick. Wide eave over roof. Three floors and a basement. Southerly pairs are identical, the northerly has ¾ round turrets to the second floor level at easterly corners, all the villas have thin balconies canopied on the east façade. Square entablatured porches at the sides. Also Northcroft Villa (77a-h) is a further development on site of the Spirax-Sarco Social Club

(a) **WOODLANDS**

(b) 1874

(c)
1858	building land sold for £1030
1876	P.H. JACKSON
1887	F. WORSEY
1905	G.G. BRODIE JP, F. WEBLEY (THE LODGE)
1928	Brigadier General E.C. PEEBLES CB, DSO, CMG, JP
1937	L.H. THATCHER (THE LODGE)

1938	East Gloucestershire Technical College
1957	A.W. HILDREW, A. TRANTER (THE LODGE) H.H. REEVE (WOODLANDS COTTAGE)
1963	demolished and succeeded by NORTH GLOUCESTERSHIRE TECHNICAL COLLEGE (principal lived in the flat, Woodlands)

(d) Seven bays. Wing gable. Five dormers. Lodge four rooms. Ornamental iron gates

(f) "Pleasure grounds 7½ acres, terraced tennis croquet lawns, greenhouses, vinery, paddock, ornamental lake[†] with boathouse, wilderness, waterfall, rustic bridges, winding walks; 16 acres of 3 well-timbered park-like pasture land" upkeep " only 2 gardeners and a cowman" – sale particulars.

[†] Hatherley brook

(g) WORSEY, bankrupted, committed suicide in bedroom; second son was killed First World War

BRODIE JP b. 1848, son of Revd Brodie rector of Down Hatherley. Managing Director of Eagle Range and Foundry Birmingham, Chairman Halford Cycle Company 1907-28. His son became Rear Admiral and Captain of Rosyth Dockyard, Commander Atlantic convoys Second World War. In 1909 as Lt RN he had made "heroic rescue of Lt Watkins when his submarine *Bonaventure* was struck by trading vessel *Eddystone*. Served till 1945 aged 61. Died 1964

PEEBLES South African War, Burmah 1891, First World War, Indian Frontier and Afghan Wars 1917-9. Second wife, Winifred, daughter of G.G. Brodie.

(h) 1854 Body of 74 year old John Davies, inmate of Cheltenham Union Workhouse was found in lake with gunshot wounds in the back of his neck; an open verdict was returned of suicide, accident or murder.

G.G Brodie and his wife at Woodlands; the Westall Brook is in the foreground beneath the simple bridge. (From a photograph circa 1920s)

PARTICULARS

OF THE VERY VALUABLE AND WELL SITUATED

Freehold Residential Estate,

KNOWN AS

'WOODLANDS'

THE PARK, CHELTENHAM.

THE RESIDENCE stands well away from the road, has a South aspect, and is of very handsome and attractive elevation. It is thoroughly well built, and is a

Country Property with all the Advantages of a Town Residence,

Situate within about a mile of the noted Promenade, Shops, Clubs, Railway Stations, and Educational Establishments. The Property is approached by a long winding Carriage Drive, with handsome Ornamental Iron Gates and Lodge (containing Four Rooms), through well shrubbed avenue, terminating on the front terrace.

THE PLEASURE GROUNDS

OF NEARLY 7¼ ACRES,

are a most enjoyable and delightful feature of the Property. They are well secluded, private, and very sunny, and have been laid out with every possible taste and discrimination. They comprise terraced shady lawns for tennis, croquet, &c., well screened and shaded by valuable shrubberies and well grown timber, kitchen and flower gardens, with green houses and vinery, small paddock, pretty ornamental lake with boat house, wilderness with running streams and waterfall, crossed by rustic bridges. The whole intersected by delightful undulating and winding walks. In addition there are nearly 16 acres divided into three very valuable enclosures of well timbered Park-like pasture land, with an Entrance from side road. The whole comprising

23 ACRES.

These Gardens and Grounds are not an expensive item in their upkeep, two gardeners and a cowman who assists, only being necessary.

N.B.—The whole of the premises are in a good state of both decorative and structural repair. Hot and Cold Water and Gas is laid on, and the house has a good complement of cupboards. All drains are believed to be in perfect order, and the premises are very dry. The Electric Light main cable is within a few yards of the house and the Electric Light could be installed at a nominal cost.

The Agents have every confidence in recommending the Property, and a moderate price will be accepted.

The Owner would consider an offer for the Residence, Stabling, Gardens, &c., exclusive of the nearly 16 Acres of Pasture Land, if a Purchaser did not require the latter.

(a) **79, ST BRELADES** and **81, RAVENSTONE**

(b) 1950s

(c) **79**, ST BRELADES
    1957   R. LEOPOLD
    1964   G. ROBINSON
    1971   Ms A. NASH
    1999*   Dr. R. ANTHONY

    81, RAVENSTONE
    1955   J. LEIGH
    1983   J. THOMPSON

    2007   sold for redevelopment of site

(d) Semi-detached pair. Two storey. (81) has an attic dormer. Centre breakforward under two hipped gables.

(a) *(SL)* **85, REDESDALE HOUSE,** 63, ST STEPHENS RD, 9 PARK VILLAS (1873)

(b) 1840-50

(c) 1871   R.S. LINGWOOD
    1876   J.F. CALLAND
    1878   Mrs S. NOYES
    1898   Major General MACDONALD
    1902   Mrs R.M. MACDONALD
    1911   F.E. HUGHES
    1921   Miss SNOWDON
    1927   H.J. LEWIS, T. MILLARIES, Mrs G.B. GOLDIE; D. LEWIS JP (REDESDALE LAWN)
    1929   LORD DULVERTON
    1933   Lieutenant Colonel H.S. LE ROSSIGNOL, Mrs PULLEN
    1936   D.D. MONRO MB, CM, C.J. RELTON, Colonel A. SKINNER DSO, OBE
    1939   Lieutenant Colonel V.A.S. KEIGHLEY DSO, MVO, Lieutenant Colonel G.A. PEAKE
    1942   Mrs V. KEIGHLEY, Lieutenant Colonel H.G.C. LAIRD DSO, Miss A. O'LOUGHLIN, Mrs C.E. SUTTON; Mrs TIDBURY (REDESDALE LAWN)

Bas reliefs inside porch, probably of Lord Dulverton and wife. He was an amateur sculptor exhibiting at the Royal Academy, so these may well be his work.

1950　　LAIRD, Miss A. O'LOUGHLIN, Mrs CROSTHWAITE, Mrs SUTTON caretaker, H.G. CONWAY (REDESDALE LAWN)

1957　　Miss A. O'LOUGHLIN Squadron Leader, C.P. BARTLETT DSO, Mrs TENCH, J. RENDLE (REDESDALE LAWN)

1961　　Miss A. O' LOUGHLIN Squadron Leader, C.P. BARTLETT DSO, Mrs TENCH, T COLLS (REDESDALE LAWN)
Conversion to flats

1999　　Ms P. ARMSTRONG

(d) Stucco over brick. Double depth plan. Three storeys: it is believed the attic floor was added subsequently. Rustication ground floor and quoining above. A central single storey porch with paired Doric pilasters and round arched windows. East conservatory bow.

(f) Gate piers at the junction with St Stephens Rd

Northcroft Lodge: SPIRAX GROUP SOCIAL CLUB converted from outbuildings 1963

R.F. SEABRIGHT

2005 Demolished

(g) DULVERTON Chairman of Imperial Tobacco Company, a Director of GWR, sculptor exhibiting at Royal Academy: the two bas reliefs inside the porch may be his work and perhaps portraits of his wife and himself

LINGWOOD Town Commissioner 1851-60, Church Warden Christ Church 1849-60. Solicitor. Bought the Lordship of Cheltenham manor 1862 for £33,000. Secured changes to the 1851 Local Government Bill and reform of the Grammar School. Opposed Public Library Act. Died 1873. A.S. LINGWOOD , son of R.S. Lingwood. born 1845. Sandhurst, resigned his commission 1867, drowned off Tenerife on the way to Buenos Aires 1870

LEWIS Managing Director of Cheltenham and Gloucester Building Society, Governor General Hospital, Commissioner Income Tax

CALLAND Magistrate for Glamorgan, drowned at Southsea when dentures blocked his windpipe; his daughter had elaborate wedding at All Saints nine carriages and four broughams, reception at Redesdale for 60 followed by ball

ARMSTRONG, broadcaster and columnist

(a) **87, HAMILTON HOUSE**

(b) Mid twentieth century

(c) 1961　　Major E.C. FISHER

(d) A terrace of three storey, brick, with an integral garage

(e) 1974　　Used as student accommodation

(a) **89, CADOGAN HOUSE**

(b) Mid twentieth century

(c) 1963   J. NELSON
    1968   A.J. GRANT
    1973   G.P. HORTOP

(d) as for no. 87

(f) as for no. 87

(a) **91, HARWOOD HOUSE**

(b) Mid twentieth century

(c) 1961   Major G.T. HARWOOD MBE

(d) as for no. 87

(e) as for no. 87

(a) *(SL)* **93/5, OAKFIELD**, 8 PARK VILLAS (1873)

(b) 1835   (second to be built in The Park)

(c) 1840   Mrs WRAY
    1847   J. HAWKES
    1850   Colonel T. FIDDES
    1870   J. GALE
    1878   Mrs and Miss GALE
    1887   -
    1891   Lieutenant Colonel SAUNDERS
    1911   Mrs PARRY
    1921   -
    1927   Mrs T. REA
    1942   J. ROBERTS, F. HILL, D. LYALL, Mrs K. PRATCHETT (owned by the Gas Board
    1950   J. ROBERTS, C. CLEEVELY, Miss RICARDO, Miss COBOURNE
    1957   J. ROBERTS, C. CLEEVELY, W. HORTON, A.G. HOLTAM
    1961   Mrs E.L. GREEN
    1968   D.R. FLINT, L.B. SHERRING, Miss E.L. STARKEY
    1971   DE SCHOOLMEESTER, L.B. SHERRING, Miss E.L. STARKEY
    1973   S. HURRELL, D. MEREDITH, G. BATE, Miss E.L. STARKEY, C. BRENNAN, J. HARRINGTON, B.L. STRANGE, E.J. WEBB, G. GILLBARD

1975   A.C. WALKER, Miss E.L. STARKEY

1999*   Five flats (93) P. BASSETT (95)

(d) Stucco over brick. Two storeys. Paired pilasters to the height of the architrave. Frieze and cornice. Windows with architraves. The outer first floor has balconies on scrolled brackets. Pierced balustrades. Central entrance porch with pairs of Doric pillars. Entablature with pediment. West side full height bow. Shutters and blind boxes

(f) Garden extended to St Stephens and Albany Roads "hot houses, vinery, peach house, conservatories, melon pits, stabling and coach houses for 4 horses" – 1863 sale/ 1849 "2 vineries each 32' long, conservatory 27' peach house 25' forcing pit." 1849 sale

3 gate piers, missing one knocked down by gasboard, cross gabled caps

(g) FIDDES was a Lieutenant General in the Bengal Army. He bought Oakfield in 1858 and was well known for entertaining. He died in 1863 and is buried at Kensal Green, London.

WRAY and daughter owners of Down's Wharf, London Land Houses.

Owner (Miss Starkey) of whole house sold off parts. The occupiers of 95, were understood to have security of tenure; but the lady sought to remove them by cutting off the water supply. The tenant (a cleric) at that time arranged for a separate supply, result the dual piping still in use.

GALE retired planter from India

(a) **97, THE MEWS HOUSE** in grounds of OAKFIELD

(b) 1850's but completely rebuilt 1970's

(c) 1970   J. MACKISACK £3250

    1997   J. ASHWORTH

(d) Detached converted coach house and rebuilt as three to four bedroom. Two storey brick on stone foundation. Stucco pedimented façade with original bull's-eye window. Pedimented porch. 1st floor arched windows and roundel in pediment. Conservatory and garage 1978

(e) Former stables and coach hose L shape structure was entirely demolished, the bricks being re-used for east boundary walk and gate piers. The reconstruction carried out by owner who bought the site in 1970

(a) *(SL)* **99, OSBORNE LODGE**, WHITE HOUSE (1916), 2, THE PARK, 7, PARK VILLAS

(b) 1833-50

(c) 1851   Lieutenant M.C. SEYMOUR RN, author
1870   Mrs SEYMOUR
1902   H.B. OSBORNE died 1905
1911   Colonel S.G.T. SCOBELL
1921   -
1927   E.W. PAYNE, Lieutenant Colonel G.A. PEAKE, Mrs PEASE
1930   E.W. GARLAND, Lieutenant Colonel G.A. PEAKE
1933   T. BOLLAND, O. WILLIAMS
1936   T. BOLLAND, D. WILLIAMS, Mrs F.W. EMERY
1942   W. LUCAS, Captain G.S. MACKAY,
          Mrs F.W. EMERY, C.H. FRY (basement)
1950   F.J. D'EATH, Major G.S. MACKAY,
          Mrs F. EMERY, C.H. FRY (basement)
1957   Mrs J.C. MILLS, F.J. CODE
1961   Miss R. BROOKE, C.S. JAMESON artist,
          J. TRACEY, C.H. FRY (basement)
1963   Mrs MUIRHEAD-TANNER,
          C.S. JAMESON, Miss PRICE
1968   Mrs MUIRHEAD-TANNER, H. MARTIN
1971   J. MARTIN

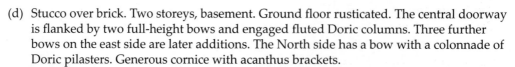

        Conversion to flats

(d) Stucco over brick. Two storeys, basement. Ground floor rusticated. The central doorway is flanked by two full-height bows and engaged fluted Doric columns. Three further bows on the east side are later additions. The North side has a bow with a colonnade of Doric pilasters. Generous cornice with acanthus brackets.

(a) **103, and 103/A,** FIRLEAZE

(b) 2006 replacing original detached two storey post WWII house

(c) 1957   A.H. CARTER MBE
1999*   Ms P. HUTCHINGS

(d) Original house suffered subsidence and drastic rebuilding but was demolished in 2005. A pair of neo-Georgian houses semi-detached. Three storeys and basement. Porched east and west arched doorway. Ground floor horizontal rustication. Concealed roof behind the parapet

(g) CARTER Assistant Chief Constable of Gloucestershire 1946-1960, having served over 40 years; died 1973

(a) *(SL)* **107, SILWOOD**, 6, PARK VILLAS

(b) 1833-50

(c) 1845   G. HYDE
    1849   Mrs S. STEVENS
    1870   Major General SHULDHAM
    1883   R. LINGWOOD
    1891   Mrs E.S. LINGWOOD
    1911   W.R. CARLES CMG
    1927   S.D. LANE
    1936   Lieutenant Colonel H.J.N. DAVIS CMG, DSO
    1942   Mrs BIDWELL, T.F. COKE, Mrs GIBBS, C.F. WEB
    1950   J.F. BIDWELL, E.W. VERNALL, Mrs GIBBS, F.T. ATMORE (garden flat)
    1957   Mrs GIBBS, A.S. BARNFIELD, Mrs MAYNE, A. VORAT (garden flat)
    1961   Mrs GIBBS, Mrs L.S. WOOD, Mrs MAYNE, D. WEBBER (garden flat)
    1968   Mrs GIBBS, Mrs SMYTHE, Mrs M. BARNETT, D. WEBBER
           (garden flat)
    1971   -
    1999*   D. FLECK, M. GRAY, J. LAUGHTON, M. CAIRNS SMITH
    2006   Ms J. SHAW-TAYLOR (Garden Apartment)

(d) With 109, a pair of semi-detached villas. Stucco over brick. Three storeys. Ground floor rustication. Doric pilasters between the upper windows. Verandah across the central windows with a lattice work balustrade and scalloped frieze. East and west entrances have recesses with Doric pilasters. Returns at ground floor have bowed breakforwards. North bow (no 107).

(f) Gate piers with pyramidal cap. Railing arrowhead and finials anthemion

(g) CARLES Vice-Consul Shanghai 1886, Acting Consul Hankow 1895, Consul-General Tientsin and Peking 1900

(a) *(SL)* **109**, RUDD HALL, 5, PARK VILLAS

(b) 1833-50

(c) 1850   Mrs M. ROLLS
    1873   Mrs STANTON
    1876   Major General SKINNER CB
    1878   R. LINGWOOD son of R.S. LINGWOOD
    1902   Mrs JOBLING
    1942   W.H. DUDLEY
    1950   Mrs F.L. DUDLEY
    1957   C.H. COUPLAND

	1968	C.J. MAYO
	1971	P.A. EVERINGHAM
	1973	C. CARROLL
	1999*	Ms N. CARROLL, P. BAKER

(d) as 107

(f) as 107

(a) **KILREAGUE**

(b) Mid twentieth century, A. ASHTON architect

(c) 1942   G.L. SCUDAMORE
    1957   W. RUST
    1999*   D. FORD

(d) Two storey, brick. North extension with swimming pool

(e) Demolished for number 115, Tivoli Mansions

(a) **115, TIVOLI MANSIONS** on site of KILREAGUE

(b) 2004 designed as flats

(d) Three storeys and basement. Five bays. Stucco. Concealed roof. Shallow breakforward centre. Porch di-style Doric, plain entablature. Horizontal rustication ground floor. Double pilasters at corners. Moulded window surrounds. Cornice. The façade to Tivoli Road has a full height bow.

(f) Hawthorn, maple, chestnut, lime felled 2007

(a) *(SL)* **123, LONGFORD HOUSE**, 3, PARK VILLAS (1873**)**

(b) 1831   purchase by Blackwell for Billings from Trye of 3¼ acre plot for FERNIHURST, but another house allowed on its south-west side; this was Longford House
    1839   Billings to Cornelius Blackwell

(c) 1840   A.K. BAKER solicitor
    1850   O. GRIMSTONE
    1851**   A.K. BAKER solicitor
    1870   Mrs BAKER
    1902   E. STEVENS
    1921   Miss B.M. HARRISON,
            Miss E.A. CARGILL
    1930   Miss B.M. HARRISON MD

1936	Miss B.M. HARRISON MD, Miss E.A. CARGILL MD
1950	Mrs VENMORE-ROWLAND
1957	P. LEWIS-DALE, R. COULSON, R.E. PAXTON
1961	P.J. SULLINGS, R. COULSON, H.L. LESLIE
1963	Misses HAMILTON, Mrs COULSON, H.L. LESLIE
1968	Misses HAMILTON, Miss PIOGNAND, H.L. LESLIE
1971	Miss K. HAMILTON, B. POULSON, H.L. LESLIE
1973	M.A. HAMILTON, M.P. ROBINSON, H.L. LESLIE
1975	M.A. HAMILTON, H.L. LESLIE
1999*	6 flats

(d) Double depth. Two storeys and attic. Stucco over brick. Pilasters to full height.

The windows on the first floor have balconies. Bow central over double door entrance. Paired pilasters with a conservatory above. The central section is higher and echoed by a bow on north.

(f) Two yews, beech and chestnut on Tivoli Road. Two pairs of gate piers with pyramidal caps for carriage sweep, also pier at Tivoli Road.

(a) **125/7, THE MEWS**, LONGFORD MEWS (1975)

(b) Twentieth century

(c)
1957	G.J.M. PEARL, W. COBB
1961	Mrs G. HARRIS, W. COBB
1968	Mrs G. HARRIS, Mrs GALE
1975	C.M. BASSET-SMITH, Mrs GALE
1979	A. LYLE to Miss C. MARSTON (Flat 1), Mrs P. MOORHEAD to D. MOORE (2)
1980	Mrs H. BANTON (2)
1994	D. GUTHRIE (1)
1999*	Ms K. GUTHRIE
2002	M. LANG (1)

(a) **129, THE COTTAGE**

(b) 1887   map suggests contiguity with 131

(c) 1903   C.M. HAWARD to J.H. HUME-ROTHERY (20 Mar)

     1903   HUME-ROTHERY to V.L.D. BROUGHTON (26 Oct)

     1936   R.M. WOODHOUSE and Ms L.F. POWER to Ms E. MATTHEWS, Ms E.K. BAYLISS and W. LEAH

     1950   Mrs S.M. GOULDING to I.M.B. JAMESON

     1957   Mrs WISE

     1961   Mrs G.A. THOMPSON

     1999*   R. GIBBONS, P.J. CONWAY

(f) 1990   The corner of the north end of the garden transferred by GIBBONS to Bob CHICK, builder.

(a) **131, THE LITTLE HOUSE**

(b) Contemporary with Fernihurst, being former stable

(c) 1903   C.M. HAWARD to J.H. HUME-ROTHERY (20 Mar)

     1903   HUME-ROTHERY to V.M.D. BROUGHTON (26 Oct)

     1936   (as for 129)

     1949   PARK COURT LTD to Miss M.D. WALDERN

     1971   Mrs A. BECHER - A. POWER

     1974   R.G. SCOTT

     1979   G. EMERY

     1987   D. HARDING

(a) **1, FERNIHURST**

(See no 39 PARK PLACE)

The Feeder Roads

I F THE VILLAS determine The Park's emphatic 'pear drop' shape, the roads leading to it act as radiating strands. They may provide links with the town in their directness, or through their intersection with other arteries. Some express, by name, affiliation: Park Place, Moorend Park Road, St. Stephens Road which was originally known as the road 'to the Zoological Gardens.'

Visually and architecturally, they act as precursors to The Park with buildings that exhibit a classical style of terrace, paired or detached villas, set back in varying degrees of generosity from the pavement. In two, Tivoli Road and Grafton Road, there is further anticipation by their trees - in the case of Tivoli Road, in front gardens, and in Grafton Road, on the verges – providing an overture to The Park's rich planting. And, to reinforce the estate's identity, there are the eye-catcher features of the gate piers closing the north end of Moorend Park Road, and the monumental tower of Cornerways for Park Place's south view.

Socially too, these roads reflect The Park's history; they have seen the same pattern of occupiers ranging from retired Army officers, colonial officials and doctors, to schoolmasters, widows and the ever-necessary domestic servants.

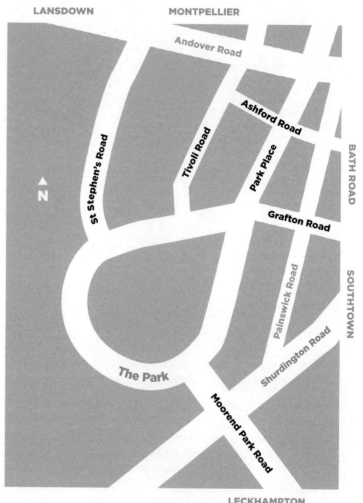

As will be observed from this basic map the principal connexion between the town and The Park is Park Place, with Tivoli Road providing a later route when it was extended; St Stephen's Road links Lansdown, and Grafton Road plays a similar role for the Southtown area around the Bath Road. These comprise the main links while, Ashford Road reflects the grid layout of development for Southtown, and Moorend Park Road represents a further association of The Park with the developing residential area of Leckhampton.

PARK PLACE

ALTHOUGH NOT THE longest of the 'feeder' roads to The Park, Park Place has maintained its Regency character in the stretch from Andover Road to Ashford Road, and fully deserves its claim to be the 'original' Park Place; the name North Road appears on later maps derived from the North Lodges, a pair of Grecian 'temples' situated where Park Gate now stands, and the final stretch to Grafton Road was Park Road as it was considered the first part of The Park. Eventually, the whole road was given the name Park Place in Merrett's map of 1834. Like The Park, building development here was slow: in the three years from 1831 only four houses had been completed; however by 1839 the street directories list thirty six.

Whereas The Park is a well-defined enclosed area encircled on all sides, Park Place is emphatically linear. Leading the eye – and the traveller – straight as an arrow through the former field layout of Lower Grotten to Cornerways' towered focus. It is a road which presents an urban overture to The Park's arcadia. For here is a coherent streetscape of closely-knit town houses: those on the east side are linked to form virtually a terrace of eight pairs with but six detached to mark intersecting roads; those on the west side show more fragmentation with only three semi-detached and just two detached corner houses. Interestingly in three cases the road junctions are not accorded single markers, but paired properties 'returned' around the corner.

And, like The Park's ring of villas, the predominant style is Regency though here many of the front doors to the pairs are set back either singly or together making for a certain monotony of facades when seen in perspective. On the east side this is only relieved by the projecting columned porches of numbers 28 and 30, fortunately four of the detached houses possessing similar features on their facades.

Of the thirty four nineteenth century buildings all but four are Listed, and to them must be added the piers, both gate and corner, together with railings, including a fine overthrow at no 19. It is to be hoped that the Listed 'bridge balustrade' outside Mercian Court will survive to mark the Westall Brook.

(a) *(SL)* **1, TUNSTALL LODGE**, 37 abuts 3 TUNSTALL HOUSE and 74 SUFFOLK ROAD, NAPIER HOUSE

(b) 1832

(c) 1871 Major DAWSON
1887 Mrs WHITLING
1891 Miss BURTON
1921 Mrs STEWARD
1927 Miss STEWARD
1930 Mrs GILL
1942 S.C. PRITCHETT, taxi proprietor, J.W. FLOOK
1950 Mrs MILLS
1963 J.H. MILLS
1965 J.H. MILLS, G. DAVIES
1968 J.H. MILLS
1999* S. BRUNT, M. LORD

(d) Recessed doorway with curving steps and niche with fanlight

---

(a) *(SL)* **2, ANDOVER LODGE**

(b) 1830 J.B. PAPWORTH "no hole more than 4' for intention of seeking spa or mineral waters, or sale of such"

1834 Lease to J. BURTON see also no 36

(c) 1850 J. BURTON
1851** no entry
1871 J.E. BATTEN
1873 Mrs COLLINS
1878 Mrs CRAWFORD
1891 Miss J. CHUTE
1901 Mrs I. MACKENZIE
1920 Brigadier General B.N. NORTH CB to C.M. HAWARD
1920 Revd L.E. GODDARD
1927 M.W. FLETCHER

1933   Mrs S.E. FLETCHER
1933   Miss E. M. COGHLAN
1934   Miss L.M. STEWARD
1937   A. BENCE
1956   A. J. PARKER
1997   M. PARKER

(d) Stucco over brick. Two storey and attic and basement. Corner pilasters. Frieze and cornice. Central entrance, distyle Doric porch with entablature including trigylphs and metopes. Windows ground floor within round-arches. Wide eaves.

(f) 1960 side land W.J. PATES

Boundary pier with pineapple finial rusticated pillar circa 1832 restored 1990.

(a) *(SL)* **3, TUNSTALL HOUSE**, 36

(b) circa 1830-2

(c) 1838   J. BURTON
1850   J.G. DA COSTA
1851** no entry
1876   J.E. BATTEN
1887   Mrs BATTEN
1927   Mrs BROKE-SMITH
1936   Miss H. STEWARD
1963   Three flats
1971   D. WEARING
1973   E. GREAVES, D.B. GODDARD, L.S. CANTY
1999* Ms C. HAYNES, J. KIVEIT, J. TAYLOR

(d) Top storey added. Three storeys and basement. Stucco. Pilasters to ends and centre of main range. Windows: ground floor architrave, frieze and cornice and boxes have double-scroll motif, basement have scrolled guards. Entrance on south set back with x-motif balustrade to side, steps to distyle Ionic porch with entablature.

(a) *(SL)* **4,** 1, PARK PLACE

(b) circa 1830-2

(c) 1851** S. WYETT, surgeon and two servants
1876   F.W. JAMES
1887   Mr COOPER
1902   F.S. GALE

1911   N.H. WALLER MA
1916   Mrs CAVE-BROWN-CAVE
1921   Mrs A.A. WEBB
1927   Miss GODFREY
1930   H.C. PENNEY
1936   Miss LEWIS
1939   Revd G.T. BERWICK curate of St. Stephens
1942   Miss E. DAWSON
1950   W.G. DASH
1957   H.J. CAMPION
1973   Dr R. HARROD
1999* J. ADAMS

(d) Pair of semi-detached villas. Stucco over brick. Hipped roof. Pilasters with sunk panel. Entrances set back: no. 4 on north side has upper floor added cornice; no. 6 has parapet, scrolled lyre motif to uprights.

(f) Area railings scrolled lozenge motif. Boundary railings have arrowhead bars and dog bars, urn finials.

(a) *(LL)* **5,** 35, THE LAWN

(b) circa 1830

(c) 1838   G. DAVIES
    1840   Mrs TULLOH
    1851** G.T. DAVIES, blind, Ms M. TULLOH and cook, housemaid, footman
    1855   Mrs Colonel TULLOH and G.T. DAVIES
    1869   C.P.A. OMAN, retired Indies planter
    1873   Mrs LAING
    1876   Captain GALE
    1887   R.E. MARSHALL
    1891   Mrs GOOCH
    1902   Mrs MONRO BRIGGS
    1915   Mrs F.E. DENIS-BROWNE
    1916   J.M. BRIGGS
    1950   Miss M.E. BRIGGS
    1965   M.M. STERN
    1999* D. BROWN

(d) Semi-detached with no 7. Original stucco villa has stone-faced square bay full height added. Extension to north circa 1900

(g) OMAN, parents of Sir Charles, also lived at 33 Tivoli Road.

(a) *(SL)* **6,** 2, PARK LAWN

(b) 1830

(c) 1851** J. WEST retired surgeon, and cook, servant, page, nurse
    1876   J. ASHWIN
    1887   T.W. KNIGHT
    1891   T.W.K. MA, tutor
    1902   K. MCLEA
    1911   Mrs D. GIBSON
    1916   W. GIBBS
    1933   Mrs GIBBS
    1936   Miss GIBBS
    1942   J.C. WOOD
    1950   Miss J. WILLIS, Miss S. BURLINGHAM, E. JONES
    1957   T. SANDERSON

(d) as for no 4

(a) *(LL)* **7,** 34, SEGRAVE (1945), MANATON (1927), ARDENNE (1921), ARDMORE (1902)

(b) circa 1830

(c) 1837   H. BRIGGS
    1851   Ms R. HILL, housekeeper
    1855   Mrs PALMER
    1871   Mrs T.W. NORWOOD
    1876   Rear Admiral MACGREGOR
    1887   Mrs MACGREGOR
    1891   Miss FORSYTH-GRANT
    1901   J.M. BRIGGS
    1911   R. GRIFFITH
    1921   Mrs DENIS-BROWNE
    1927   Mrs DAVIES
    1945   S. GOBOURN physiotherapist
    1976   P. GOBOURN
    2003   Mrs E. GOBOURN

(d) as for no 5

(f) Coach house for 2 cars. Wellingtonia; layout of garden largely as in 1855 Town Survey

(g) BRIGGS, artist and friend of Gainsborough's daughters, through them acquiring their father's watercolour paint box and some of his works which he bequeathed to his niece Mary Clarke

S. GOBOURN, blinded in World War 1 when a soldier

P. GOBOURN, son of S. Gobourn; Cheltenham College. 1942 Cameron Highlanders, post Second World War RASC and Royal Corps of Transport, retired as Major, became MBE; Chairman and President Cheltenham Branch Royal British Legion; County Commissioner for St John Ambulance 1984, invested as officer of the Order 1986; president Cheltenham Rotary Club 1990. Died 2003.

(a) *(SL)* **8,** 3

(b) 1830-2

(c) 1833   Mrs DWARRIS
1851** Mrs BAINES and Mrs G. MAKENZIE, and three servants
1871   Misses HOLME
1873   Mrs BRIND
1891   Mrs F.H. CRAWFORD
1902   Mrs MARTIN
1921   Mrs E.F. WICKSEY
1950   A. ST. G. EDMONDS
1957   D.H.S. RUSHER
1959   Mrs F.P. HANKINS
1973   F.L. TRAVIS
1975   D.M. TRAVIS
1999* Ms F. WHITTEN (8B)

(d) Pair of semi-detached villas. Stucco over brick. Hipped roof. Wide eaves to centre, low parapets to end bays. Entrances north and south conjoined to neighbours.

Windows: ground floor have guards with embellished lattice motif, north porch fanlight with Gothic glazing bars.

(f) Area railings scrolled lozenge motif; steps railings have arrowhead, bars and dogbars with urn finials.

(a) *(SL)* **9,** 29, MANDEVILLE COTTAGE (1828)

(b) 1825   P, ROCK builder

(c) 1851** Mrs WESTROPP, two servants
1871   Mrs PRESGRAVE

1873   Revd A. ORMEROD
1876   Mrs LAING
1887   Mrs G.A. BAKER
1921   A. BAKER
1927   F.G. PERKINS
1930   A.K. PRIDAY JP
1950   Mrs L.H. LAWFORD
1959   Mrs R. MILLER
1961   five flats including Mrs MILLER
1971   four flats
1975   Mrs MILLER, Miss I. COLE,
          F. WAIND
1999* five flats

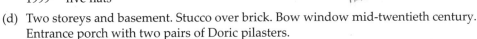

(d) Two storeys and basement. Stucco over brick. Bow window mid-twentieth century. Entrance porch with two pairs of Doric pilasters.

(g) WESTROPP seems to have lived at the former no 33 in 1840, but its location is hard to identify; similarly R.G. WHATLEY is recorded at no 32 in 1838 but where it was is elusive.

(a) *(SL)* **10**, 4

(b) 1830-2

(c) 1851** Misses S, M, and L. BINGHAM and two servants
     1921   Miss PLUMER
     1927   A.V. ARMSTRONG
     1959   Miss E. ARMSTRONG
     1999* Ms S. JOHNSON

(d) As for no 8

(f) As for no 8

(a) *(SL)* **11**, 28, MORAY CROFT (1916)

(b) 1828-30

(c) 1851** Mrs CRUTTENDEN and three servants
     1855   Captain COUSINS
     1871   Mrs Col STEVENSON
     1878   C.T. BLANSHARD
     1887   L.C.F. ELLIS
     1891   E. CLEEVELY traveller
     1902   Mrs D.M. GARDNER

1911　J. MACAULAY
1916　Miss DUNCAN
1927　Miss G.H. MOULDER
1963　H.E. CLAPP
1971　V. AUSTEN
1999*　P. LEIGHTON

(d) Pair semi-detached villas. Two storey. Central four window range breaks forward. Doric pilasters with incised Greek key motif. Entrances within porches with Doric pilasters with incised Greek key and anthemion motif. Fanlight bat-wing and circle. Wide eaves. Long balconies with circular web, scroll and anthemion pattern.

(f) Octagonal capped gate piers with finial; double iron gates, ornate spearhead bars, ramped up to ends.

(a) *(SL)* **12,** 5

(b) 1820-32

(c) 1840　Captain HAMILTON RN
1851**　Misses FITZMAURICE, T.F. SCOTT and wife, and two servants
1873　C.H. JESSOP solicitor
1902　HYLTON JESSOP
1930　Miss G. GILLETT / GILLIAT
1939　Miss A. HART
1950　Miss G. GILLIAT
1999*　J. FENTON, and three flats

(d) Pair of semi-detached villas. Stucco over brick. Hipped roof. Two storeys and basement Pilasters sunk panels. Tooled first floor band and frieze. Entrance set back at north and south each. Fanlight north Gothic glazing bars, south margin lights and lozenge motif. Porches lozenge scrolls to upright ironwork. Parapets above porches. Windows have iron balconies ground floor. Abuts no's 8 and 10

(f) Railings to steps arrowhead with bars and dogbars, urn finials.

(a) *(SL)* **14,** 6, THE LAWNS

(b) 1823

(c) 1838　J.B. MORTON
1850　Mrs Colonel HEWISON
1855　Mrs FISHER
1871　Mrs MEREDITH
1873　Miss MORGAN

1887	Miss SWETE and Miss MILES
1902	F. GASTRELL
1911	Mrs E.V. PEEL
1921	Mrs HATHERN
1933	Misses MOORE
1959	Misses MOORE, Mrs H. BOURNE
1961	Mrs S.M. FOULDS
1970	C.S. MARTYN

(d) Central front path moved to side, as for most of the terrace; garage in basement under kitchen which was "once a Roman Catholic Chapel" – Ms Foulds. The north light to this has stained glass depicting Saints Joseph and Mary, though central panel of Christ was given to St. Stephen's church by Miss Foulds.

Kitchen range in basement; fine sash boxes and matching door surrounds, elaborate vine cornice plasterwork.

See no 12 for architectural description.

(a) *(SL)* **15**, 27, WALTON HOUSE

(b) 1828-30

(c)
1838	R. COMFIELD
1850	Mrs Colonel TENNANT
1851**	Mrs M. MONRO, daughter and two servants
1855	Misses HULL
1871	Miss M.A. WILSON
1873	Mrs WILSON
1887	Mrs A. SMITH
1902	C.J. PHILLIPS
1911	D. MALLORY
1916	Ms GIBSON
1921	T.F. COKE
1927	Mrs LUCKMAN
1942	Mrs E.M. HINGSTON
1957	C.H. ROBERTS, F. HALL
1959	Mrs L. ROBERTS, F. HALL
1961	Miss M.R. VIEL, Mrs E.M. BRABBIN
1963	A. GREEN
1968	C. GREEN
1973	J.T. MURLY

(d) As for no 11, also stone balcony short bulbous balusters.

(f) Gate piers as for no 11, and railings to step have x-motif.

(a) *(SL)* **16,** 7, BRYANSFORD HOUSE (1911)

(b) 1830s after J.B. PAPWORTH, architect

(c) 1840   T.M. DA SILVA
    1851** Major LEIGHTON and two servants
    1873   Major LEIGHTON
    1878   Miss LEIGHTON
    1911   Revd T. KEANE
    1921   Mrs KEANE
    1942   Miss M.M. BAILEY, Miss D.M. CROSS, Mrs E. STILL
    1950   BRYANSFORD PREPARATORY SCHOOL
    1957   BRYANSFORD PREPARATORY SCHOOL,
             Miss M. BAILEY, Miss D. CROSS
    1963   Miss D. CROSS
    1968   Miss CROSS, H.W. DAWSON (16A)
    1975   Miss D. CROSS
    1982   DAVIES, builder to G. BREEZE

(d) Ashlar over brick. Hipped d/pitch roof. Two storeys with basement and rear attic. Ground floor rustication, Tuscan pilasters. Porch Doric columns in antis. Entablature with triglyphs and metopes, iron bootscrapers. Wide eaves.

BREEZE was curator of Cheltenham Art Gallery and Museum, unsurprisingly he had frontage window frames painted in nineteenth century colour.

Conservatory now the kitchen.

(f) Gates and piers with R. DAY incised are probably original and were recovered from back garden, while railings found in front garden served as model for replicas by Marshalls.

(a) *(SL)* **17,** 26, COLONSAY LODGE (1921) ST. ANDREWS LODGE (1911)

(b) 1820-32 G.G. PAINE £1,100

(c) 1832   T. WILLIAMS, C.G. THOMAS and G.G. PAINE
            to J. MORTON
    1838   Lady VANE
    1843   Mrs M.A. ROBERTS
    1851** J. WILSON retired barrister, and three servants
    1855   Mrs PLACE
    1871   A.I. SCOTT
    1876   Mrs GATHORNE
    1878   J.B. FOLLIOTT
    1902   G.A. GRIST
    1911   Revd W.H. JELLIE

1913   A.M. ROBERTS surgeon, to Miss MITCHELL
1936   E. MACNAMARA
1939   Mrs MACNAMARA
1950   D.C. DUNDAS
1957   H.B. TRUSCOTT
1958   Lady M. DOWTY £2,550
1961   Mrs D.M. FELL, 'Sir G. DOWTY's sister'
1973   BALLADOLE ESTATES LTD, Isle of Man £10,000
1984   Major J.S.M. EDWARDES £68,000
2004   S.R. DAVIES and Ms S.J. CREESE £530,000

(d) Pair of semi-detached villas (with no. 19). Stucco. Two storeys and basement. Pilasters with incised Greek key motifs. North extension has particularly attractive glazing bars of Gothic idiom.

(f) Gate pier pair ashlar with Gothic panels and stepped capping 1820-32, nineteenth century iron gates.

(g) WILLIAMS owned land and house on south side; PAINE on north side "no wells to be sunk for medicinal water or salt, no noisome, offensive trade or business." MORTON also owned St. Oswolds, Tivoli Road. His lease was one year to avoid stamp duty.

(a) *(SL)* **18,** 8, ST MARY'S RECTORY (1975)

(b) 1830s after J.B. PAPWORTH, architect

(c) 1838   Major-General PODMORE
    1851** R. LAMBERT, four children and one servant
    1873   D. LITTLEDALE
    1887   Captain ROSS
    1891   Miss MARWOOD
    1902   Mrs SMYTHIES and Mrs LARDEN
    1916   Mrs SMYTHIES
    1927   W. SMYTH MB CM (retired)
    1933   Mrs SMYTHE
    1939   Mrs E.C. PRICHARD
    1950   G.B. MATTHEWS, physician and surgeon (surgery)
    1975   G.S. BOLAN, Revd G. HART
    1994   Revd T. WATSON, rectory for St. Mary's till 2004

(d) Ashlar over brick, d/hipped roof. Two storeys with basement and rear attic. Ground floor rustication. Pilasters incised decoration. Porch with two pairs of Ionic columns, frieze and pediment, fanlight circle motif.

(g) LITTLEDALE devised lettering for the blind, 1838 (see 39, Tivoli Road)

(a) *(SL)* **19,** 25

(b) 1820-32

(c) 1838   Mrs TINLING
1850   Lieutenant Colonel TINLING
1851** R. CLARKE shoemaker, and adopted child
1855   Mrs PICKERING
1871   Miss PICKERING
1873   Admiral HARDING
1887   Mrs PICKERING
1891   Miss HILES
1911   A.H. WYATT
1916   Mrs COLQUHOUN
1927   H.A.C. COLQUHOUN
1930   Mrs EDEN
1933   Mrs CADDELL
1942   Colonel D. HARTLEY
1950   Mrs HARTLEY
1957   Major S. HILLS
1959   Mrs E.A. MAKIN-SMITH
1961   Mrs E.A. MAKIN-SMITH, Mrs E.M. STEVENS (19a)
1963   Mrs E.A. MAKIN-SMITH, Mrs C.M.B. OHLSON
1971   C. MARECHAL, Mrs OHLSON
1973   C. MARECHAL, E.M. COLE
1999*   Five flats

(d) As for no 17, with centre bay set back. Doric porch with two pairs of columns, entablature with triglyphs and metopes, fanlight batwing and circle.

(f) Gates, railings and, particularly, lamp overthrow with scrolls and square holder.

Gate piers scrolled lozenge and peaked caps with urn finials.

(a) *(SL)* **20,** 9

(b) circa 1832

(c) 1840   Miss SINDERBY
1851** E.W. JOSEPH and two servants
1871   Ricardo LINTER
1873   Miss GREEN
1902   Miss UNDERHILL, Misses LEY
1916   D. COGHLAN
1936   Miss L.A. COGHLAN

1965   Miss COGHLAN, J.J. STANTON, Miss GREENSLADE
1968   Miss COGHLAN, Miss P, J.J. STANTON
1973   Miss COGHLAN, J.J. STANTON, K. KORCYNSKI
1975   Miss COGHLAN, K. KORCYNSKI
1999*   D. JARVIS

(d) Pair of semi-detached villas. Stucco over brick. Hipped slate roof. Recessed entrance bays at sides conjoined to neighbouring villas. Pilasters through ground and first floors at ends and centre. Fanlights. Window guards on ground floor scrolled lozenge motif, oval and quatrefoil frieze to porch.

(f) Railings

(a) *(SL)* **22,** 12 (1850)

(b) circa 1832

(c) 1838   Mrs REID and daughter, maid and cook
    1840   Mrs YOUNG
    1873   Miss LONSDALE
    1891   Miss C.H. JAMES
    1911   Miss JAMES and T.E. TRELEAVEN
    1916   Miss JAMES
    1927   Miss M.E. HOWELL
    1933   W.A. FINCH
    1957   A.G. CUMMINGS
    1975   A.F. FULLER, L.M. WARREN
    1999*   L. MENATO

(d) As for no 20, but no frieze to porch. Lozenge motif to sides of steps.

(f) Railings

(a) *(SL)* **24,** (13) BENTLEY HOUSE (1891)

(b) 1825 G. PAINE and P. ROCK land for £600 from T. HENNEY and J. BROWN plasterer, sell to J. HALL for £310 but no's 24 and 26 not finished till Oct 1826 by another builder, J. CLUTTERBUCK

(c) 1842   Lady CECELIA LA TOUCHE
    1851** Mrs PHAYRE five daughters, two servants
    1855   Miss CHAPMAN
    1871   Sir F. FRANKLAND Bart
    1878   W.F. HEATHER
    1883   E. PHILLPOT bequeathed to Mrs PHILLPOT
    1915   A.E. SAUNDERS for £270

1921 Mrs K.M. PEEBLES tenant
1925 MULHECUN tenant
1933 Revd D.F.J. DAVIES
curate of Christ Church Chapel, tenant
1937 H.E.A. WAKEFIELD, tenant
1949 Captain R.W.V. REEVES RN
1957 Mrs K. LAVICK, Miss K. WRIGHT
1957 Misses CRAIG £3,150
1968 Ms E. MINSHULL
1973 E. MINSHULL
1975 P.E. MINSHULL
1999* P. VAUS primary school head retired

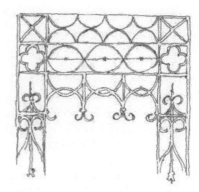

(d) Pair of semi-detached villas. Stucco over brick. Two storeys. Entrance bays set back at sides conjoined to neighbours. Pilasters at ends and centre. Decorated first floor band and crowning frieze both with anthemion motif. Entrance: fanlights radial glazing, scrolled lozenge motif to uprights and oval open work friezes. Individual balconies with double-scrolled lozenge motif to ground floor.

(g) FRANKLAND probably related to Whinyates family of Pittville.

(a) **25,** (24) HOUSE (1911), BEDFORD VILLA (1871)

(b) Mid nineteenth century

(c) 1851** H. MACLAINE or MACLEAN and servant
1871 Mrs E.B. ALLEN
1876 Mrs LUARD
1887 Mrs HUMPHREYS
1921 J. HADDEN (see 6, Ashford Road)
1971 E.A. SMITH, B.J. CLUTTERBUCK
1973 E.A. SMITH
1999* J. EDMONDS

(d) Plain stucco villa. Two storeys.

(a) *(SL)* **26,** (14)

(b) As for no. 24

(c) 1838 W. ISAACSON, J. TURTON
1840 Miss LLOYD
1842 Misses COMYN
1851** Mrs Colonel STEVENSON, widows pension,
from Bombay. Daughter, son and two servants.

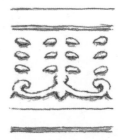

1862   Mrs HOOLE
1871   Mrs MORGAN
1878   Mrs GOLLAND
1882   Colonel BELL
1900   T.W. MITCHELL
1910   Miss GRANT
1921   Mrs HUGHES
1927   Miss GRANT
1939   Misses PHILLPOT
1950   Miss PHILLPOT
1965   Miss JAMES
1971   L.I. DAVIDSON, M.E. CADLE
1975   L.I. DAVIDSON
1999* J. JONES

(d) As for no 24

(f) Railings arrowhead

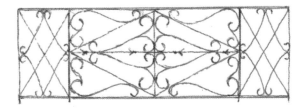

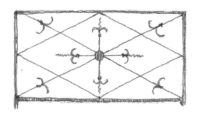

(a) *(SL)* **27,** (1916), BONNIE DOON (1916), BEDFORD VILLA (1911), 23, BEDFORD HOUSE (1871)

(b) circa 1832

(c) 1838   Miss PAUL
     1850   Mr KING, Misses COMYON
     1851** H. KING lodging house keeper
     1871   Mrs THOMPSON
     1902   Miss DUNN and Miss CHETWYND
     1916   Mrs DICKSON
     1927   Miss M.G. HILL
     1957   Miss L. ALLIES
     1959   Miss L. ALLIES; Miss E.C. MCEWAN
     1971   Miss MCEWAN
     1999* Ms J. BALLINGER, N. MCCORDALL

(d) Pair semi-detached included no. 6 Ashford Road. Two storeys and basement. L-shape plan. Stucco over brick. Pilasters sunk panels end and centre. Entrance projecting porch. Pilasters incised decoration, batwing and circle fanlight, sides to steps x-motif balustrade. Basement window guards embellished sticks.

(f) Pier at corner with Ashford Road.

(a) *(SL)* **28,** 15 KINGSDOWN (1921)

(b) 1825-32

(c)
1838	Miss AIREY
1840	W. BELL, surgeon
1851**	Mrs H. BELL, two scholars and one servant
1855	C.F. COOKE
1876	Miss TAYLOR
1878	Mrs BABINGTON
1891	W.H. HART
1902	F. GORDON-ALLEN
1911	Mrs TAYLOR
1916	Misses FRY
1921	Mrs E. WEBSTER
1927	F.W. ECROYD
1936	G.W. BRACE
1939	Mrs M. BRACE
1942	R.J. DARCH-STUCLEY
1950	H. STEPHENS, Mrs WALKER
1957	I.G. TRACEY, G.J. MORGAN
1959	I.G. TRACEY, K. DAVIS
1961	I.G. TRACEY
1965	L.R. GIBBONS, G. WILLIAMS
1968	L. SMITH, G. WILLIAMS
1971	E.I. THATCHER, G. WILLIAMS
1973	G.M. LEWIS, F.G. FINDON, G. WILLIAMS
1999*	I. TRACEY

(d) Pair of semi-detached villas. Stucco over brick. Two storey and basement. Horizontal rustication to ground floor. Pilasters at ends. Paired entrances at centre, tristyle Doric porch entablature with triglyphs and metopes, side balustrades scrolled lozenge motif.

(f) Railings

(a) *(SL)* **29,** PARK PLACE, PARK END (1, PARK VILLA) on site of Lower Grottens field

(b) 1833   W. MONTAGUE and C. CHURCH to J. LEA

(c) 1838   D. JOHNSTON
   1840   J. WYATT surgeon
   1847   Miss S. DORVILLE
   1878   Mrs D. LATOUCHE and Miss ST. GEORGE
   1887   Mrs E. MACREADY
   1891   Mrs PRANCE
   1898   J. LEA, Ms M. ROGERS, £884
   1902   Surgeon Major General BROKE-SMITH, £1,100
   1911   Dr A.F.R. CONDER
   1927   Miss E.C. JOHNSON
   1928   Lieutenant G.F. JOHNSON, £1,500
   1930   Mrs G. LLOYD
   1937   Mrs G. LLOYD, B.B. WALLER, Miss E.K. BAYLISS
   1940   A.B. CRUIKSHANK, A.L. RIDE, £1,000
   1945   M.T. AUDSLEY civil servant, W. RUST, £2,350
   1950   T.W. RUST
   1956   L. HIDDLESTONE civil engineer, £4,250
   1957   B. HUDSON
   1959   B. HUDSON, L. HIDDLESTONE
   1961   I. OUSMITH administrator, £5,400
   1963   S.A. ROBINS, B. HUDSON (basement)
   1967   E.L.G. ROBINS, £6,500
   1973   Mrs J.N. CHAMPNERS, £23,000
   1978   Mrs M. TAYLOR, £53,000
   1987   J. ALLEN, £261,000
   1999* J. ALLEN, Ms A. BRUNSKILL, D. HYPHER, Ms V. MCMILLAN, Ms E. WELLER
   2001   M. SILVA neuro-surgeon, wife radiologist

(d) Stucco over brick. Concealed roof. Two storeys and basement. Pilasters at ends. Central distyle. Ionic porch with entablature. South conservatory by 1919.

(f) No 33 built in garden. Garage at back replacing front one 1998. Corner piers at Ashford Road, "good feature with 6, Ashford Road" - *SL*, ashlar pillar incised panels with anthemion motif. Railings.

(a) **30,** 16

(b) 1825-32

(c) 1838   Misses PEMBERTON
   1871   Miss PEMBERTON
   1876   Mrs DICKEN

1887   Miss HILES
1891   Mrs LAWSON
1902   Miss M.A. TYNTE
1921   Misses WHITTARD
1942   Miss L. WHITTARD
1957   Mrs J.E. ETCHATS
1968   W. KEELING
1973   J.R.S. BROWN
1999*   R. JOHNSON

(d) As for no. 28

(f) Railings

(a) *(SL)* **32**, 17

(b) circa 1826-32

(c) 1840   Misses PEMBERTON
1851**   Mrs NEWBURY / NEWBERRY and nurse, cook
1876   Mr JAMES
1878   J. GOLDINGHAM
1887   Mrs H. WOOD
1891   Miss DICK
1902   S. WILLIAMS and Revd J. FISHER-JONES
1911   Mrs MACNAIR
1916   Miss FERGUSON
1927   Mrs DUNCOMBE
1930   Mrs MONEY
1939   Mrs F. PUDDICOMBE
1957   C.E. MACKENZIE
1963   Mrs MACKENZIE
1971   E. PRICE
1975   S. WEARE
1999*   Ms S. STITT

(d) Pair semi-detached villas. Two storey and basement. Stucco over brick. End entrance bays set back, fanlight radial glazing, pilastered surround with dentil frieze.

(f) Railings urn finials

(a) **33**

(b) 1980s, in garden of 29

(c) 1999*   J. WILDEN

(f) Detached. Two storey. Rendered villa.

(a) *(SL)* **34,** 18

(b) 1826-32

(c) 1850   Mrs C. PALMER
     1851** Mrs E. BARNARD seamstress
     1855   Mrs L. WILLIAMS
     1871   Captain C. HENRY
     1887   Mrs RYAN
     1891   Miss M.A. RYAN
     1911   Miss D. WILKINS
     1921   W.B. BUSH
     1927   Misses KIRKLAND
     1961   Miss B. KIRKLAND
     1963   Mr KULENKANIPFF
     1965   Mrs KULENKANIPFF
     1968   R.F. TREHARNE
     1973   C.R. THOMPSON
     1975   D. DYER-BARTLETT
     1999*   F. RUSSELL

(d) As for no. 32 but no radial fanlight glazing

(f) Area railing with three levels of bars

(g) HENRY see Hanover Court, St. Stephens Road

(a) **35**

(b) 1954

(c) 1961   C.A. PENBERTHY
     1971   D. PENBERTHY
     1999*   J. ROBINSON

(d) Detached. Brick. Two storeys

(f) Mature chestnut tree

(a) *(SL)* **36,** 19

(b) 1825   G.G. PAINE and P. ROCK builders on Lower Grotten land

(c) 1836   R. SALMAN, deceased
     1840   Captain ALEXANDER RN
     1850   E. ALEXANDER
     1871   W.F. HEATHER
     1878   Miss SCOTT

1911   Mrs MANN and Miss E. GRIFFITHS
1916   J. CAWOOD
1921   H.E.A. WAKEFIELD
1937   Revd R. TYNDALE (curate St. Philip and St. James)
1942   T. PEARSON
1950   Mrs PEARSON
1963   Miss BOWEN, St. Mary's College
2006   D. MOSS and S. BAYLISS

(d) Attic common with three adjacent houses. Pair of semi-detached villas. Two storeys and basement. Central pilaster sunk panel. Entrance at side conjoined with neighbour, porch pilasters and dentil frieze.

(a) **37,** MERLES CLOSE (1984)

(b) 1959   On land formerly part of grounds of FERNIHURST sold by C.M. Haward to A. Rogerson of FLEURVILLE Ashford Road for £400; on Rogerson's death sold to W.J. Peacock for £1,125

(c) 1959   PEACOCK to E. STONE £700 to J.B. SAVERY £3,500
1961   Commander P.F. TROLLOPE RN Rtd. (works manager) £4,500
1963   A.G. BUTLER, ARICS £5,500
1974   A.B. ASPEY £20,500
1984   C.J. DINGLEY £115,000
1985   D.R. THOMAS HM Inspector of Taxes £100,000

(d) Bungalow, brick with detached garaging
1981   Extension of 1,000 sq ft £13,300

(f) 1979   Enlargement of garden by purchase part of rear of 1, Ashford Road for £2,500

(a) *(SL)* **38,** 20

(b) 1835

(c) 1840   Mrs COMPTON
1850   Mrs W. TUSTIN
1851**   W. TUSTIN builder, W. HEATHER
1855   W. HEATHER
1871   W. TUSTIN
1876   Miss BOULTER
1891   Mrs MORRIS
1902   Mrs LAMBERT
1927   Miss LAMBERT
1936   Miss A. BAKER
1942   Miss E.H. KESTEVEN

1950   Miss E.M. CROWTHER

1999*   M. MAWER

(d) As no 36 and porch has scroll motifs to uprights, openwork frieze and x-motif.
Balustrade. Blind boxes.

(f) Railings

(a) **FERNIHURST,** 2 PARK VILLAS (1873), BOTELER HOUSE (1841), VIRGINIA WATER
(1833)

(b) 1831   H.N. TRYE sold for £375 land to C. BLACKWELL to build house acting for
T. BILLINGS junior, 1833 TRYE bought back house called 'Virginia Water'
for £5,500

1841   TRYE sold BOTELER HOUSE to C. COLCLOUGH for £3,990 with extra land
for £500

(c) 1838   J. STOCKWELL

1841   C. COLCLOUGH

1850   Mrs COLCLOUGH

1851** Ms A. LANE housekeeper

1870   J.P. HAINES JP

1879   Major General J. MUSPRATT-WILLIAMS

1911   Colonel H. STEWARD

1916   J.S. HAWKINS

1921   E.H. CRAWSHAY JP

1927   Miss L.F. CRAWSHAY

1939   Miss E.K. BAYLISS, C.B. DOBELL

1942   Miss E.K. BAYLISS, C.B. DOBELL, Captain C. BIRD, Colonel C. HARDINGE

1950   Miss E.K. BAYLISS, A. ANLEY, Mrs MCCASH, Major W. HILL

1957   PARK COURT LTD

1959   Demolition

(f) 1833 grounds included two lakes and were fronted on Park Place with a balustraded
bridge of 1833 over the Westall Brook; kitchen garden with coach houses, stables. By
1901 grounds had been extended from half an acre to two and a half.

(g) CRAWSHAY related to R. CRAWSHAY 'iron king of Wales' who died at Queen's Hotel
1879.

CAESAR COLCLOUGH was from County Wexford

MUSPRATT-WILLIAMS born 1832, died 1901. Indian Army; married widow of
Rear Admiral CUMBERLAND. Gave statue of Christ to St. Stephens, churchwarden
1884-93. Hosted many garden fêtes and shows. Son of chaplain to East India Company.

(a) **39,** PARK HOUSE

(b) 1963   Redeveloped Fernihurst site for 15 flats, enlarged in 1971 to 30 flats

---

(a) *(SL)* **40,** (21)

(b) circa 1820-32

(c) 1850   Mrs D. HARRINGTON, widow of Captain HARRINGTON, East India Company
    1873   Mr HALE
    1891   Mrs HINGSTON
    1902   Mrs SMITH
    1911   W. SMITH
    1927   Miss S.A. SMITH
    1950   H.G. DOXSEY
    1957   A.G. SMITH
    1959   Mrs F.E. SMITH, Mrs F.E. LUMBY
    1963   Mrs LUMBY, Mrs F.E. SMITH
    1975   J.E. LUMBY
    1999*   C. ROBINSON

(d) Pair semi-detached villas (with no 8 Ashford Road). L-shape plan. Stucco over brick.
    Two storeys and two storey entrance bay set back. Central pilasters with sunk panel.
    End entrance conjoined with neighbour, fanlight, uprights scrolled and openwork frieze
    Veranda x-motif balustrade and fretted timber uprights.

(a) 22

(b) 1830s

(c) 1850   Miss ADDISON
    1851** Miss M. BARLOW, Miss S. EDEN, Miss A. DORVILLE, Miss E. STOODLY, friend
    1855   Mrs R. CROSSE
    1871   Mrs HALL, Miss ROCK
    1873   Miss ROCK
    1876   J. SIMMONS
    1878   Miss PLACE
    1891   J.M. TEAGUE professor of music
    1921   Mrs JOHNSON
    1927   G.E. MOON
    1930   H.L. MALONE

            Absorbed/demolished with expansion of Majestic Hotel

(e) 1851   census suggests two separate households each having a cook and housemaid.

(a) **NETHERMUIR**

(b) 1834

(c) 1850   L.H. KING, Miss COMYON
    1902   J.H. HAY
    1921   Miss WARD
    1927   Mrs APPS
    1930   Lady GREY
    1932   demolished

(d) 1835   North Lodge and School House and yard extending south to Segrave House rear

---

(a) **MAJESTIC HOTEL** on the site of NETHERMUIR

(b) 1832   incorporating consulting room of J. CARPENTER, osteopath in Ashford Road

(c) 1932   Miss E.K. BAYLISS; private hotel

(d) 1934   renamed HOTEL MAJESTIC and extended to 48 bedrooms
    1955   E.A. WILKINSON manager (see FLEURVILLE, ASHFORD RD)

(h) 1989   vacant; demolition following fire

(a) **PARK GATE**

(h) 1991   complex of flats on site of MAJESTIC HOTEL

PARK GATE

(a) *(SL)* **46** MERCIAN COURT - YWCA - PARK COURT (1959) HEIGHTHORNE (1891), SEGRAVE VILLA (1851), 1, SEGRAVE HOUSE (1834)

(b) 1834   to include 'ornamental lodge' on field called Heighthorne Heydon, T. BILLINGS

(c) 1938   W.M. BEETLESTONE
    1841   Revd J. BALFOUR
    1842   T. BILLINGS
    1843   Miss BELL
    1846   Miss DORVILLE
    1851** Mrs A. DOUGLAS 75 year old annuitant, her sister, two daughters and four servants
    1870   Captain A.J. FLEECE RN

1873	G. RUSSELL and W. GUY to Ms M.S. RUDD
1876	1) Mrs H. RUDD 2) Mrs CHAPMAN
1878	Captain MAGUIRE
1884	Revd P.H. WORSLEY and J.W. RUDD to Admiral H. CHRISTIAN
1887	Misses GILEY
1891	Colonel G.F. BLAIR RA
1902	Admiral CHRISTIAN
1927	Colonel D.C. CARTER CB, CMG
1959	YWCA Miss F.E. ROWE warden
1984	Retirement Home 38 apartments resulting from combining numbers 46 and 48
1887	extensions

(d) Stucco-concealed roof. Three storeys and basement. Ground floor rustication. Paired pilasters at end and centre. Centre bay is two storeys. Entrance north end.

(e) 1841 boarding school, BALFOUR headmaster and four children, governess, four servants, two assistant masters, twelve boys 10 -15yrs.

1956 school for girls again?

(f) Road boundary has balustrade surviving from Westall brook bridge 1833.

(g) CHRISTIAN 1858-61 commanded HMS *Euryalus*; 1861-3 RY *Victoria and Albert*; 1865-1910 Chief Constable Gloucestershire, Admiral 1889, MVO 1909, reputedly related to Fletcher Christian of *Bounty* mutiny.

Ornamental lodge (b) was moved in 1850 by T. Billings to be a spa building at The Park.

(a) **48**, MERCIAN COURT, SEGRAVE VILLAS (1851), 2, SEGRAVE HOUSE (1834)

(b) South half of building

(c)

1842	Miss BELL, annual lettings
1843	Mrs H. FORMBY
1846	Dr H.C. BOISRAGON, G.P. MASON, Mrs LLOYD
1851**	Ms M. FISON governess and eight scholars
1874	G. RUSSELL and W. GUY to H.T. CHAPMAN
1898	F. GOLDSMITH et al to R.W. HELLINGS
1899	G. HERBERT
1902	Mrs HARDIE, Mrs H.B. HENDERSON (at no. 1?)
1921	S. GOBOURN CSMMG, ACBM masseur

Mercian Court with the bridge balustrade marking the Westall Brook

(d) As for north half

(e) 1841 school see 1, Segrave Villas

    1851 school boarding, 8 girl pupils and governess, cook and 2 maids

(g) BOISRAGON Physician Extraordinary to George III, leading Mason and notable person in town's cultural life, with brother had practice at 11, Royal Crescent 1841, and at 14 Bayshill Terrace 1846. Died in 1852 at Bideford, Devon.

(a) *(LL)* **50,** PARK HOUSE WEST (1942), GLENARBUCK LODGE (1921), WESTBOURNE LODGE

(b) 1851** 'building' but apparently little development till 1858 when land auctioned and bought by C. RAINGER builder for £445 (including Heysham House plot) and made over to C. BIRD builder.

(c) 1870   Mrs HAMILTON
    1902   Misses HAMILTON
    1927   Misses MOORE
    1930   A.C. ALLEN
    1933   MRS FLETCHER
    1942   Miss E.K. BAYLISS at service flats
    1957   PARK COURT LTD service flats
    1961   T. TAYLOR et al
    1971   four flats
    1973   A.J. BOWRING, flat four
    1990s   Renovation

(d) Detached villa. Two storey and basement and attic. Centred bay ground floor coined corners. Entrance porch at south with tower, blind first floor window. Extended on south east.

(f) Driveway shared with Heysham House till 1990s.

(a) *(LL)* **52,** HEYSHAM HOUSE (1980), HANDSWORTH LODGE (1860) from Birmingham birthplace of the Whatelys

(b) [See Park House West for shared early history]

    1831 covenant between H.N. Trye and Henney and Brown that any buildings on the site i.e. Heighthorne, Heyden Mowing Breach and Rough Breach of the Grafton Estate should be of ashlar or cement and blue slate.

(c) 1861   Misses WHATELY (6) from Eton Lodge, The Park
    1891   Misses WHATELY (2)
    1895   E.H. TAYLEUR from T. WILKINS for £1,500, who had himself paid only £970 at auction four months earlier

1901	Mrs S. TAYLEUR
1902	J.H. HAY
1906	F.L. SCHUSTER
1907	Seven year lease £85 pa
1930	Mrs SCHUSTER
1936	Miss SCHUSTER
1950	Misses SCHUSTER
1951	Swansea Baths and Laundry Co.
1952	Leased as four flats:
	A.C. IMPEY £3,750
	Ms E.B. FOWKE £3,250
	Ms E.B. FOWKE £1,900
1957	R. BRITTON; Mrs HARVEY
1959	R. BRITTON; Mrs HARVEY; Mrs H. GILL
1961	R. BRITTON; Mrs HARVEY; Mrs H. GILL; Mrs SMYTH
1971	J. GRIFFITHS; Mrs P. VEVERS; Mrs HARVEY; P. SMITH
1999*	Four flats

(d) Two storeys. Three bay facades on west and south with attic and basement. Ground floor windows have architraves. Quoins at corners. Bracketed eaves under slate roof. Side entrance on north with later porch on Grafton road façade.

(g) SCHUSTER retired wealthy shipping merchant from Manchester, died 1928. House left to son Claude, first Baron Schuster GLB, CVO, KO, JP permanent secretary to Lord Chancellor 1915-44; director Legal Division Allies' Control Commission for Austria; mountaineer, Vice President Alpine Club 1937; daughter Elizabeth married T.F. Turner QC Recorder of Rochester, (see also 32, St. Stephen's Road).

TIVOLI ROAD

CALLED "PRESTIGIOUS" by estate agents, "a particularly attractive environment" by a Department of the Environment inspector, and "fashionable" by Victorian guide book writers, Tivoli Road is arguably one of Cheltenham's most engaging thoroughfares.

Laid out in the 1830s on land called Marybone Park by developers Thomas Newman and Thomas Hale Bennett, it was extended to join The Park when the Westall Brook was culverted; the resulting curve in direction is anticipated by the reduced front gardens of 35 to 41 on the west side and the set back of 41a to 45 the result of a former nursery here. The other villas on this side have created a sense of wideness by their generous front gardens, partly because from 1 to 25 their backs are restricted by the ancient Tivoli Lane; while those on the east side enjoy generous rear gardens from 2 to 16 with access to Andover Walk.

Architecturally, there is a consistency of style - seen also in The Park's villas - with main floor windows under recessed arches and porches rich with classical detail. Even where the house is smaller scale - as at 15 - the idiom is retained. However, recent building, mainly on the sites of the two nurseries and where demolition of original properties has taken place, does not contribute greatly to the quality of the road.

Perhaps 'quality' could be applied also to the road's social history. Since Victorian times the occupants here have included military high-rankers, doctors, explorers, actors, musicians, diplomats, scientists, academics, even a princess.

But what contributes most to the character of the road is not just the architecture or society, but the planting: trees in front gardens, sited near to the pavement and showing a rich variety of scale and species; hedges rather than sterile brick walls or, worse, wooden fencing; substantial shrubs rather than fussy flowerbeds; and, above all, no sacrifice of garden to meet the demand of the motor car. It is a vulnerable, fragile ambience, wholly dependant on house owners' sensitivity to the value of streetscape quality and a willingness to replace natural decay and depredation. Such is the big responsibility and indeed privilege to maintain this "particularly attractive environment".

(a) *(SL)* **ST JOHNS LODGE**, TIVOLI CIRCUS, 92, SUFFOLK RD, 27, ANDOVER RD

(b) circa 1820-50

(c)   T. BENNETT land £310, Revd J.K. FOSTER tenant
        A. HARTLAND
  1853 Prince CAULKER lodger
  1870 Lady STURT, Captain Sturt (son)
  1887
  1960 Miss A. NICHOLLS of Gers, France, CLARKE, NICHOLLS & MARCEL tenants: consulting engineers

(d) Ashlar over brick, with south extension now separate, stucco.

Two storeys and basement, pilasters at corners and centre. Ground Floor windows have Doric pilasters, as also centre entrance. Crowning entablature has parapet scrolled motif and heavy brackets.

(g) CAULKER, West Africa prince brought to Cheltenham by Countess of Huntingdon Missionary Society and lodged here 1853 by Revd J. Foster; throne of Bompey usurped during his six year stay; became blind.

STURT was permitted by Queen Victoria to adopt the title even though her husband Charles died before the accolade of knighthood could be bestowed for service in Australia (see also no 33)

(a) **HARLEY LODGE**, (Suffolk Road from 1961), CROSSWAYS (1930), 1823 BROCKLEY VILLA after Brockley Park Ireland

(b) 1820s

(c) 1823   Revd T. KEMMIS
  1851** H. DAVIES
  1861   H. DAVIES

1881**   uninhabited
1891   Mrs P. BENDALL
1910   Mrs BROKE-SMITH
1925   W. BAGULEY
1930   G.H.R. FAWCETT
1933   W. BELL-HAWORTH
1936   Mrs H. BELL-HAWORTH
1942   Mrs H. HAWORTH
1950   Miss N.A. COLSTON
demolished 1950s because
of A40 widening

(d) Villa stucco over brick. Two storeys.
Pilasters each end of main three bay block.

One storey south wing, interrupted cornice over canopied verandah with ironwork supports. North two storey wing, similar east porch on square columns with incised anthemion head panels, entablature.

(g) BELL-HAWORTH former master at Cheltenham College, moved here from Cornerways, The Park.

DAVIES purchased 36 Gratton Road (Greville Lodge) in 1867 but did not live there.

(a) *(SL)* **1,** LYNDON LODGE (1881), 2, TIVOLI VILLAS (1874) , 2, TIVOLI COTTAGES (1858), 1 TIVOLI VILLA (1851)

(b) 1834

(c) 1837   Captain HARRISON
1838   H. DAVIES owner
1842   Mrs SIMONS
1847   H. DAVIES owner
1847   Mrs DALZELL
1848   Mrs PRATT tenants - T.H. BENNETT - Mr KEMPSON, Mr STATHAM, Mr READ, Mrs A. SIMONS
1849   Mrs Colonel ROSS
1850   J. AINSWORTH
1851   Mrs HOBSON
1852   J. HATCHETT
1853   Mrs HULL
1856   Lieutenant Colonel SPARROW
1858   J. HERBERT ironmonger; £550 at auction
1865   Captain LONG
1860   B. EVANS

1862   H. CLIFFORD
1870   Madame DU BEAU
1875   Mrs PARKER
1879   J. RAINBY dealer in bric a brac
1883   Mrs WRIGHT tenant
1884   Mrs L. ALLEY
1885   Mrs STENHOUSE
1890   J.F. SADLER grocer at 24 Andover Rd
1930   Mrs E. MANN
1957   H. MANN
1961   H. MANN, D.B. SIDGWICK
1968   H. MANN
1979   R. PUGH furnishers "Lyndon Designs"
1988   C.N. SILLS builder

(d) Two storey villa. Stucco over brick. Horizontal rustication with voissoirs over windows.

Central bay slightly recessed. Entrance on north with tent porch having scrolled bracket supports conservatory extension 2005

Office annexe on north for MANN and Co. Tivoli Coal Exchange

(e) 1869-74 Madame Du Beau's Academy for Young Ladies

(f) Rowan

(g) A. MANN coal merchant

(a) *(SL)* **2,** WALCOTT HOUSE (1940), EARLSTON (1894), 1, SALOPIAN VILLAS (1847) TARLOGIE LODGE EAST (1836)

(b) 1836   J. FEARN

(c) 1839   Revd H. SMITH
      1841   Mrs S. HAWKINS
      1842   J. BROWN
      1843   Lieutenant Colonel KIRBY
      1845   H. PARKER
      1846   Sir H. GRAHAM
      1847   Mrs J.H. MURRAY
      1858   Mrs MURRAY, Miss PELHAM
      1861   Major General LAWRIE
      1865   Mrs BEHAN
      1867   Mrs CRASTER
      1876   Miss CRASTER
      1886   Miss HAYES

1888   Colonel F.F. BAINBRIDGE
1894   Revd Dr. W. MACGOWAN
1929   Revd H. COURTNEY
1930   Mrs E.S. COURTNEY
1933   Miss E. COURTNEY teacher of dancing
1957   Miss COURTNEY, Miss E. COURTNEY-BOYD
1963   Miss COURTNEY, Miss E. COURTNEY-BOYD,
        E.F. YOUNG ARICS, A.I. Arb
1968   Miss E. COURTNEY-BOYD
1971   L. SANDHAM, R. NEWTON, M.H. YATES
1973   L. NEWTON, R. NEWTON, S.J. GEORGE
1975   L. NEWTON, P. STAIGHT, D. BRAVEN
1979   M. BOOTHMAN
1981   Mrs A. HUGHES of Astley Nursing Home
2000   Ms J. CHARLTON (3) T. & S. JOHN (5) R.G. TURNER (6)

(d) 1836 "two elegant uniform villa residences" drawing room and dining parlour each 20" long, 6 bedrooms, servants hall, kitchen, basement offices, cellars. Downstairs two rooms curved inside walls and doors. Pair of semi-detached villas, ashlar over brick, two storey and basement. Central range canted forwards and porch further with shared tristyle Doric under entablature. Balcony has scrolled lozenge ironwork. Horizontal rustication to ground floor surmounted by modillion band

(e) 1985 converted to six flats

(f) Large fig tree removed and curved section of back squared to make patio

(g) MACGOWAN master Cheltenham College

COURTNEY-BOYD name change with inherited castle in Ayrshire

BOOTHMAN managing director LinotypeHell moved to 35, The Park

(a) **3a**, REGENCY COTTAGE, TIVOLI VILLA (1851) 2, TIVOLI VILLAS (1847) 2, TIVOLI (1834)

(b) 1833

(c) 1834   KEMPSON
     1847   Mrs M.E. DALZELL, Mrs A. SIMONS
     1851   Mrs A. HOBSON
     1858   Mrs WARNER
     1859   Mrs GILL
     1860   B. EVANS
     1862   H. CLIFFORD surgeon

1950   Mrs B.T. MCLAUGHLIN
1968   D.B. SIDGWICK
1999*   Mrs J. SIDGWICK

(d) Divided from no 3 between 1945 and 50. Ground
     floor verandah glazed roof. Iron uprights with
     quatrefoil and anthemion panels. Scrolled
     openwork frieze

(f) Cut leaf beech, prunus

(g) SIGWICK administrator Sudeley Castle

(a) *(SL)* **3,** GREYSTONES (1910), IVY LODGE (1851), IVY COTTAGE, TIVOLI VILLAS
     (1847), 3, TIVOLI (1834)

(b) 1833

(c) 1833   W. ROSSITER to Ms E. GREGORY: W.R. HARRISON tenant;
     1834   HADLEY
     1839   Ms AINGE
     1846   Mrs THOMAS
     1850   Captain N. JONES
     1860   Mrs HAND
     1865   Revd J. WATSON
     1870   Major A. FITZJAMES
     1870   Colonel FITZJAMES
     1871   Mrs S. PEARCE
     1879   Miss GRETTON
     1880   Colonel JOHNSON
     1881** Ms E. SOWNDES plus four Johnsons (children of parents elsewhere)
     1884   Dr BAXTER
     1890   Mrs H.T. MONK
     1893   J. MOORBY
     1896   Mrs K. FLETCHER, Ms F. FELTON
     1901   Mrs C. PURDON
     1910   Revd J.F. CORNWALL
     1928   Lieutenant Colonel E.O. SMITH and Major F.W. FEATHERSTON-GODLEY
     1930   Mrs E.M. GODLEY
     1939   Mrs SISSON
     1940   G.M. GILL
     1945   Mrs R.C. PRICE
     1950   Lieutenant Colonel H.K. NEWSOM
     1953   A.D. HAY
     1956   Mrs G. HAY

1975   R.D. O'NEILL
1994   A. COMPTON

(d) Stucco over brick. Two storeys. South bay set back. Horizontal rustication ground floor with vousoirs over windows. 1st floor outer incised Greek key surround, centre window in arched recess. centre porch solid pilasters with balcony scrolled lozenge motif

(f) holly

(a) *(SL)* **4,** MELMERBY (1930), CORFIN (1919), SALOPIAN VILLAS (1858) the Brown family had association with Lydbury, Salop, WALCOT HOUSE (1842), TARLOGIE LODGE WEST (1836)

(b) 1836   land sold 1833, house pair (with no 2) to J. BROWN £1450

(c) 1841   J. BROWN
     1847   Major J. BROWN
     1858   Mrs A. BROWN
     1882   Major General A. BROWN £400
     1891   Miss A. BROWN, F. HARMAN BROWN
     1919   D. LEWIS £550
     1929   Mrs N. ASTON
     1930   H. LEWIS (son) £700
     1930   Mrs H. CRAIG
     1936   W.J. CRAWHALL
     1942   Miss M.A. CARBONELL
     1950   J. DUCKER, J.E. DUCKER, Mrs G.E. COURT
     1955   Mrs O. GORMAN £2,500, N. DONIACH £3,125
     1957   N. DONIACH
     1961   N. DONIACH, A.J. LUCK
     1963   P. PARKINSON, J.B. WIDDOWSON, A.J. LUCK
     1966   CHELTENHAM BRIDGE CLUB £6,000

(d) Pair of semi-detached villas with no 2. Ashley over brick. Two storey and basement. Central range canted forwards and porch further with shared tristyle Doric under entablature. Balcony has scrolled lozenge ironwork. Horizontal rustication to ground floor surmounted by modillion band.

(e) reputed use of basement as synagogue 1995

(f) silver birch felled 2007

(g) Major J.H. BROWN. adc to "Clive of India", Deputy Lord Lieutenant of Shropshire (hence house name) daughter Adelaide lived and died here 1909

WIDDOWSON master at Dean Close Junior School

D. LEWIS Cheltenham C&G Building Society

DONIACH – GCHQ

(a) *(SL)* **5,** (27), MARYVILLE 4, TIVOLI VILLAS (1847) MARYVILLE (1840)

(b) circa 1830-40

(c)
1839	Lieutenant Colonel J. HARRISON
1840	D. CURLING
1841	Mrs TATHAM, Mrs LONG
1853	Mrs REYNOLDS, Mrs COOOMBES
1858	Mrs COOMBES
1860	Mrs WALLER
1881	Mrs E. PRINGLE
1891	Miss PRINGLE
1865	Mrs DIGGLE
1865	Mrs HARDY
1869	Revd J. WOOD
1867	Mrs HARDY
1871	Revd. H. DRAPER
1910	Commander----
1929	Lieutenant Colonel W.K. HATCH IMS
1939	Mrs HATCH
1950	Miss MCVICAR
1955	Prince G. IMERETINSKY
1963	G. BARLOW
1968	Prince G. IMERETINSKY
1975	Princess M.V. IMERETINSKY
1991	Mrs K. BARKER
1994	Mrs R. MILLS
2002	S. FOX
2005	Mrs FOX

(d) Villa stucco over brick. Two storeys. Single bay set back north, full height canted bay to south. Horizontal rustication ground floor with voussoirs over windows. First floor centre window in arched recess. Blind boxes. Central entrance solid porch. Pilaster and entablature. Balcony ironwork heart and honeysuckle motif.

(e) 1869-74 private boarding house for Cheltenham College

(f) cut-leaf beech, two firs, laurel

(g) IMERETINSKY, Prince George godson of Tsar Nicholas II of Russia, his father member of Imperial Guard; fled at Revolution; Grenadier Guards; married Nancy 1933; died 1972; widow died 1990

(a) *(SL)* **6,** TIVOLI LODGE (1837)

(b) circa 1820-34

(c) 1834   Mrs HARMER
     1837   Captain MANLEY, R.N.
     1844   Mrs HOLT
     1846   J.S. RODNEY
     1858   J. BEALES
     1861   Mrs BEALES
     1865   General FABER
     1868   General T. POLWHELE Bengal Infantry
     1891   Mrs C. CARBONELL
     1910   Misses CARBONELL
     1924   J.D. LOVELAND, E.E. BIRD
     1929   H. JORDAN
     1939   Mrs JORDAN
     1942   Misses JORDAN
     1950   D.M.J. DAVIDSON
     1954   Misses TRAFFORD
     1961   Misses TRAFFORD, E. ROBINSON
     1968   Misses TRAFFORD, E. ROBINSON, D.A. HEWITT-JONES
     1973   Misses TRAFFORD, D.A. HEWITT-JONES
     -----   S. WILKINSON
     1993   S. TAYLOR

(d) Villa. Ashlar over brick. Two storey and basement. Ground floor windows in arched recesses. Central porch, Doric pillars, entablature with wreaths. "Tivoli Lodge" on south ground floor. Railings each side of porch have ornate scrolls

(f) sycamore, lime, fir, yew

(g) Captain MANLEY acted as Master of Ceremonies at Montpellier Rotunda 1833-4

     TRAFFORD sisters: 1966 &1975 legacy to Cheltenham Arts Council "to advance education by promotion of music and the arts"

     HEWITT-JONES Director of Music Dean Close Junior School, Deputy County Music Adviser, composer; wife cellist and composer

---

(a) *(SL)* **7,** TIVOLI HOUSE, TIVOLI VILLAS (1847) TIVOLI HOUSE (1839)

(b) 1833   W. ROSSITER to J. BATTEN

(c) 1838   Mrs BURTON
     1841   T. BARTLETT

1844	Misses HAVELL
1847	R. WOODWARD
1853	P. SMITH tenant
1854	J. ALLIES
1858	W.H. ALLIES
1861	Revd R. THOMPSON
1862	Mrs CHRISTOPHER
1869	Revd J. WOOD
1871	Revd H. DRAPER
1875	Mrs L. PARKER, widow and widowed daughter, son
1883	Ms L.S. ALLEY
1885	Mrs BROOK
1896	Mrs ARNETT
1898	W. CAMPBELL
1910	Mrs MOTTRAM
1923	D. LEWIS
1929	Mrs H. TAYLOR
1936	Mrs ROTHWELL, Mrs GRASSBY
1937	Mrs D. PAYNE
1942	A.W. PAYNE
1950	E.L. HOARE
1957	R.L. BRAMWELL
1975	J. MARTLEW solicitor

(d) Villa. Ashlar over brick. Two storeys. Corner pilasters. Horizontal rustication.

Ground floor windows have incised voussoirs. Entrance at south end set back with Doric pilasters. Wide eaves. First floor band inscribed "Tivoli House".

(e) 1869-74 private boarding house for Cheltenham College

(f) magnolia, acer, leylandii front hedge

(g) ALLIES antiquary FSA, special interest Herefordshire and Worcestershire

HAVELL teacher of French, Italian, History, Geography; drawing from nature and perspective

---

(a) *(SL)* **8,** TIVOLI LAWN (1847), TIVOLI HOUSE (1840), ST JAMES HOUSE (1834)

(b) 1834   M. BARRETT builder

(c)
1840	Miss MATTHEWS
1842	R.S. LINGWOOD owner, Revd J. BALFOUR tenant
1847	J.R. CAMPBELL
1858	Mrs ALLEYNE

1859   Mrs BELL
1860   Sir J.J. REID
1865   Mrs M. DALZELL blind
1874   Ms E. WAKEMAN owner
1881** Mrs LITTLE, Mrs E. CRECK
1878   Mrs S.F. LITTLE, Mrs E. GATHORNE
1896   Colonel GOLDSMITH
1910   Mrs KEMPTON
1931   J.B. LUTMAN
1931   Mrs LULMAN
1951   Miss E.K. BAYLISS £33,000
1957   J. GILTHORPE, E.F. YOUNG, Miss MCKINNON
1961   YOUNG, MCKINNON, G. HUBBARD
1968   ROBOTHAM & YOUNG quantity surveyors, G. HUBBARD
1971   ROBOTHAM & YOUNG, D. ROWLAND, H. MCCRAE
1973   D.P. ROWLAND
1975   P.T. JONES
1987   D. SWEPSON optician
1999* Dr. E. RICE-EVANS garden flat
2004   P. SLABBERT

(d) Villa. Stucco over brick. Two storey and basement and attic. Pilasters to south.

Arched recesses over ground floor windows. Central porch Doric pillars; architrave wreathed, stick balusters, wreathed handrail to steps, facade similar to No. 6.

(f) silver birch, holly, yew

(g) REID Chief Justice of Corfu, son Robert MP for Hereford, Dumfries, Solicitor-General, Lord Chancellor, Earl Loreburn; lake in Canada named after him.

(a) *(SL)* **9**, (6) THE FOLLY (1978), ST OSWALDS, 6, TIVOLI VILLAS (1847)

(b) 1833   T.H. BENNETT stonemason £157.10 land, sold house for £804

(c) 1833   J. MORTON
    1840   Ms C. MUNTZ
    1843   Lieutenant Colonel P. WILLETS
    1856   C. BROUGHTON
    1876   W. SMITH builder £600
    1879   Mrs C. AYLMER widow
    1877   A. TERRY, Mrs HOWIE
    1898   Miss CHAPMAN
    1899   Lieutenant Colonel CAMPBELL
    1905   Mrs W. MURPHY
    1908   W. SMALL £400

1910 Colonel CONDER
1920 Mrs H.L. LANGSTON £800
1950 Captain E.T. EVANS £2,350
     H.W. SHAKESPEARE, C.H. GRANT
1957 A.S. LANE £2,000
1961 C.H. STOATE
1963 M. RYAN
1975 G. CLARIDGE £19,000
1975 Tape Maintenance Ltd, M. RYAN,
     R. STOATE
1978 A. NINER £27,500
1989 T.M. DEY £342,440

(d) Villa. Ashlar over brick. Two storey and basement. Regency Gothick in Strawberry Hill Style. Stucco detailing. Hood moulds to windows, octagonal and stepped buttresses capped by castellated finials; similar for central porch with traceried entablature over four-centred arch. Breakforward bays each side and crowning frieze has idiosyncratic pediment tracered heads to all windows with heraldic panels beneath ground floor ones

(f) laurel, maple, beech

(g) WILLETS served in Peninsular War alongside MONRO of 11 Tivoli Rd

CONDER born Cheltenham explored Palestine for Ordnance Survey, his grandfather married granddaughter of Roubiliac sculptor

---

(a) *(SL)* **10**, ST JAMES VICARAGE (1930), HARCOURT LODGE (1861)

(b) circa 1856

(c) 1856 Mrs C. ANSON
    1860 T. RAMSDEN
    1861 Mrs RAMSDEN, Mrs M. MORGAN
    1865 Major General POLWHELE
    1867 Captain HOPKINS
    1871 Mrs S. HOPKINS
    1878 J. HENDERSON
    1879 Mrs SEALY
    1881 Mrs HOPKINS
    1883 Mrs SEROCOLD
    1885 Mrs S. HOPKINS
    1898 Major PIERS, Mrs P. MORRIS
    1901 Mrs DE COURCEY, F. GRAHAM
    1910 Mrs CRICKET
    1929 Revd G.M. BOOTHROYD Vicar of St James

1936   Revd A.D. LUKYN-WILLIAMS
1942   Revd E.J. ELDRIDGE OBE
1968   R. BERGMAN
1980   M.B. JONES cardiologist

(d) Villa. Stucco over brick. Two storeys and basement. Doric pilasters to breakforwards.

Windows under arch recess ground floor, architraves over first floor. Wide eaves. Central entrance, ashlar Doric portico paired columns, triglyphs and metopes entablature, stick railings to steps.

(f) holly, yew

(g) ANSON related by marriage to General Sir George Anson, MP for Lichfield and Governor of Chelsea Hospital; Admiral Baron G. Anson wrote "Voyage Round the World" (1748)

(a) *(SL)* **11,** (7) CHARNES (1920), LANG SYNE (1891), 7 TIVOLI VILLAS (1881), TIVOLI WEST (1873), 7 TIVOLI (1841), 6 TIVOLI (1839), TIVOLI (1837)

(b) 1834   T.H. BENNETT £175 land

(c) 1837   F. MONRO
1881   Miss M. MONRO
1900   Miss S. TAYLOR, A. RICHARDSON
          tenant till 1911
1920   Mrs A. YONGE £275
1929   Dame S.J. BROWNE,
          Miss H. HOOLE £950
1942   Miss H. HOOLE
1972   D. ROWLES

(d) 1834 villa. Ashlar over brick. Two storeys and basement. Pilasters at corners. Windows have arch recess ground floor, sliding shutters. Centre porch. Square Doric columns, balcony above a scrolled lozenge motif.

(f) Chestnut (young Richardson's hiding spot to mystify passers by). Cornelian cherry. Iron gates

(h) MONRO related to Dr. Monro, physician to George the Third; friend of Gainsborough, Turner and Cotman

RICHARDSON art master at Cheltenham Ladies College. Father of Ralph, actor, born here 1902

BROWNE First President of Royal College of Nursing. DBE, RRC

(a) *(SL)* **12,** FAIRHAVEN (1929), THE MOORINGS (1897), BURWELL LODGE (1861)

(b) circa 1834-40

(c)
1856	Mrs A. DOUGLAS
1876	C. WILKINS
1879	G.W. CALDWELL retired India Civil Service
1883	General HATCH
1886	W. CADELL
1890	General HATCH
1891	C. MELLOR
1893	Major WYLEY
1901	Mrs A. PRITCHARD
1910	Miss JARRATT
1929	Colonel A.S. PEEBLES
1939	Mrs TURNER-MILLER, E.B. MCLEAN
1942	D. CALDER, L.C. ALLTON, E.B. MCLEAN
1950	Four flats
1961	W.J. MARTIN, M. SWORDS, Misses POWELL
1968	Five flats
1975	T.J. BYRNE
1999*	12 flats

(d) Villa. Stucco over brick. Two storeys and basement. Corners Doric pilasters.

Wide outer breakforwards. Ground floor recessed windows under arches, blind boxes and 3 level boxes Central porch. Two pairs Doric columns, entablature triglyphs and metopes. Wreathed handrail.

(f) prunus, holly, hawthorne

(a) *(SL)* **14,** BAY TREE HOUSE, 1, DELABERE VILLAS (1851)

(b) 1839 G.G. PAYNE bought land

(c) 1840 R. NEWMAN builder; sold unfurnished houses via Simonet and Whatley to J. WILLIAMS builder in 1850; sold them 1851 to W. CHARLEWOOD as 2 Delabere Villas.
1852	Miss COUNTESS
1858	Mrs MITFORD
1859	Mrs H. MACINTYRE
1860	Gen HOLLES
1861	J. KILLIE
1871	Misses HALIBURTON
1874	Dr TURNBULL
1881	Mrs A. DAY
1886	Major General ELGEE

1891   J. DICKINSON
1893   Revd A. GARDNER
1901   Mrs M. WEBSTER
1930   Mrs S. PASCALL
1942   Miss M.I. PASCALL
1950   L.S. PASCALL
1968   J.A. EASTWOOD
1971   Ms M. CREWE
1975   V.J. STRATTON, A.T. ADAMS,
        P.J. ST JOHN
1988   J.M. FOX
1996   Mrs W. CEDERHOLM

(d) A pair of semi-detached villas with no 16. Stucco over brick. Two storeys and basement. Doric pilasters including pair between parties. Windows ground floor under recessed arches. End porch Doric pilasters. Stick balusters. Ground floor balconies embellished oval motif.

(f) holly, prunus

(a) *(SL)* **15,** (8), MYRTLE LODGE (1929), MYRTLE VILLA (1881), LASSINGTON VILLA (1851)

(b) circa 1834-40

(c) 1851   Ms M.A. ADDIS (born in Lassington)
     1858   Mrs EVERS
     1863   Miss BENNETT
     1861   Mrs N. EBERE
     1862   R. TIBBLES
     1865   Mrs PHILLIPS
     1868   Mrs OVERBURY
     1879   L.J. MACDONALD, Major J.B. FENNELL
     1887   Revd S. WADE
     1907   auctioned
     1910   Mrs GIBSON
     1929   Miss A.E. BARKER
     1971   V.F. REES, P.M. REES, C.R.H. JACKSON
     1975   V.F. and P.M. REES, C.R. JACKSON
     1999* R. DEAN

(d) Villa. Stucco over brick. Two storeys with a concealed roof. Centre breakforward.

Corner pilasters. Windows arch recesses. Centre solid porch. Pilasters.

(f) Maple

(a) **16,** ALEXANDER HOUSE (??), 2 DELABERE VILLAS (1881), CHARLEWOOD (1857)

(b) (see 14 for early history)

(c) 1840   R. NEWMAN
1850   J. WILLIAMS
1853   Colonel HANDCOCK, Revd W.F. HANDCOCK
1860   L.W. HARRISON
1871   Misses BLAND
1889   Miss DICKERSON
1891   Mrs J. DICKINSON
1891   General ELGEE, J. KELLIE
1899   Mrs J. MULLETT
1925   Mrs A.G. LONGMAN
1930   F.W. LONGMAN
1933   F.W. LONGMAN, Revd F.H. PATON
1936   Miss DAVIS, Revd F. PATON
1939   Mrs M.V. MONTAGU (1), W. LONGMAN (2), Miss E. EARÉE (3)
1942   Mrs G.B. ENNIS (1), Miss E. EARÉE (2)
1950   Mrs J. LISTER (1), Miss E. EARÉE (2)
1959   M. JONES (1) P. HAYDON
1961   Mrs B. WALLIS, P. HAYDON
1971   B. WALLIS
1975   A.W. RODGER
1996   Respite home A. ELBANNA

(d) As for no 14 extension with to south

(f) Sycamore, lime

(a) **17,** on site of LONDON NURSERIES (1891)

1862   Land sold by W.H. HENNEY to Miss E. DOUGLAS £162.10
1881**   uninhabited
1891   MOORMAN AMDS
1910   Misses NORMAN
Land sold for building

(c) 1961   Miss A.E. BARKER to T. SOWCROFT
1968   Miss M. PRINCE
1973   S.M. PRINCE
1999*   Ms J. HECQUET
2001   Ms K. BARKER £182,000
2004   Professor P. CRALL

(d) Brick. Two storeys; tiled hipped roof

(g) CRALL Professor of Education, Reading University

(a) *(SL)* **18,** NORTHUMBERLAND LODGE (1851), TURBERVILLE LODGE (1841)

(b) 1839   E. TURBEVILLE LLEWELLIN and R.B. MITFORD
of Mitford Hall, Morpeth, Northumberland

(c) 1841**   Captain CHURCH RN
1848   H. BUCKLE
1858   B. MITFORD
1881**   B. MITFORD Civil Service Cape of Good
Hope, and son at Durham University
1891   W. M. POOLEY dentist
1897   A. ROGERSON
1901   Mrs F. MILNER, tenant
1908   E. OSBALDSTON-MITFORD, £1,750, owner
1910   Miss YOUNG, tenant
1929   Mrs THORNHILL, tenant
1930   Mrs WOODHEAD, owner
1933   Major General Sir R.O. STUART KCSI, RA
£2,200
1949   W. BULLINGHAM et al to N.W. LOVELOCK
1951   T.W. PALK, £3,650
1996   Mrs M. MALLEN
2001   R. YOUNGS, surgeon

(d) Villa. Stucco over brick. Concealed roof. Two storey plus basement. Horizontal rustication. Voussoirs and arches ground floor. Central breakforward. Corner Doric pilasters. Centre porch paired Doric columns. Entablature triglyphs and metopes.

1949 division of 18 Northumberland Lodge and Fairmile House

(f) Wellingtonia 80', 3 limes bordering Ashford Rd

(g) B. MITFORD proposed system of reading for the blind 1864

STUART Director General of Ordnance, India, d.1948. brother-in-law of Field Marshal Lord Birdwood

PALK descendant of Sir Robert Palk Governor of Madras 1763-7; Project Manager of Spirax Sarco; MBE for service to Admiralty 1962

(a) *(SL)* **18a, FAIRMILE HOUSE** (1950) a division of no 18

(c) 1959   R. BARRELL

      1961   D. CUTHBERT
      1963   D.L.G. CREWE
      1968   T.D.L. HERON court registrar, Gloucester, Air Commodore CLAYTON
              A.M. SMITH dentist
      1980   M. BOSS
      1985   D. MESSENGER
      2006   K. ORCHARD

(d) Incorporates south bay of no. 18, with doorway 2007 pilasters and entablature

(f) willow felled 2003, prunus substitute

(a) **18 1/2, CUMBERLAND LAWN** (1949)

(b) 1839

(c) 1930   E. WOODHEAD
     1950   G.G.C. KING
     1960   E.M. WOODHEAD
     2009   J. RICKARDS

(d) Coach house for number 18 converted by Strickland; wing and garage 1950. Bargeboards. Verandah east side

(f) South east corner of garden 150 year holm oak, cypress. South area sold 2005 as a building plot where Mitford Lodge now stands; Benchmark on base of entrance wall 218.5

(g) KING building inspector for Cheltenham

     E.M. WOODHEAD patents attorney for Dowty

(a) **MITFORD LODGE**

(b) 2006   architect: Ylangou Associates; builder: Lightmoor

(c) 2006   C. JONES, R. MALPASS

(d) Neo-Georgian villa. Two storey and basement. Entrance north corner

(f) Holme oak in rear, Scots pine, yew felled 2005

(g) JONES retired NHS manager psychiatry

     MALPASS retired visual designer for Cavendish House department store

---

(a) **18b PENN HOUSE** (1939)

(b) 1939   W.J. PATES (see Cedros Lodge)

(c) 1939 Mrs W. PENN RICHARDSON
1942 Mrs C.H. RICHARDSON
1953 Ms J.M. CAMPBELL £2,500
1953 A.J.H. MASTERS £4,000
1964 G.D. MEADOWS £5,850
1979 Receiver to J. DELL £36,000
1984 USA company executive of aircraft subsidiary (TRW PROBE later TRW Electrical) in Cirencester
1988 Land auctioned for £121,500: equivalent to £730,000 per acre to CLARKE WEST builder
1990 house demolished and new build G.S. BOLAM to J. BRISTOL surgeon
1997 P. JACOBS £220,000

(d) Brick. Two storey. Corner quoins. Integral garage. Hipped roof.

(a) **19,** on the site of LONDON NURSERIES (1891)

(b) 1967 Charlton Kings Builders

(c) 1967 C.G. FLETCHER

(d) 1982 loft conversion with conspicuous dormers

(f) Poplars on west boundary. Two apple trees and pear tree presumably survivors from nursery, all felled. Front garden emphatically hard surfacing and rigid symmetry

---

(a) **20,** CEDROS LODGE (1920) PENTLAND (1901) ALBA VILLA (1881)

(c) 1859 Major General J. BRETT £2,200
1868 Captain WALDY
1869 General SHUBRICK
1871 Mrs J. BRETT
1898 Colonel TYLER
1899 Revd H. GIRDLESTONE, Major A.F. MOCKLER-FERRYMAN
1901 Mrs J. MOCKLER
1910 Mrs OERTON
1914 F.C. RYND £450
1920 Captain G.R.F. TAYLOR £1,150, Miss FLETCHER
1920 Mrs L.M. GREIG £1,500
1933 Miss M.S. BAYLEY
1938 L. HANSON to W.J. PATES £341 plumber and decorator
demolished 1939 replaced by 18b PENN HOUSE and 20 THE FIRS

(g) J. BRETT East Indies Service

(a) **20, THE FIRS** (1942) on site of CEDROS LODGE

(b) 1939

(c) 1939   Mrs M.A. STORRAR
    1944   J. WILSON £2,500
    1968   Mrs I.C. WILSON
    1980   Mr LONG £25,000
    1981   I.M. WILSDON
    1999   D. HOLLAND

(d) Two storey rendered on brick. Breakforward north of centre door. Extension to south converting d/garage into office with first floor build comprising bedroom et al.

(f) Silver birch killed by brick wall, felled 2007. Scots pine felled 2005

(h) 1996 featured in TV serial "Next of Kin" with Penelope Keith and William Gaunt

(a) *(SL)* **21,** (10) RISDON (1936), POWISLAND VILLA (1881)

(c) 1858   Revd G.W. CHAMBERLAIN curate of St. James
    1885   Major GEN. RICH
    1890   Mrs M.A. HARNETT
    1901   Mrs C. MEDLEY
    1910   Major GILBERT
    1929   Mrs E.O. GROWSE
    1933   Mrs FERGUSON
    1936   Mrs E. DAY
    1950   Miss E.K. DAY
    1957   H. DAY, Miss DAY
    1961   Mrs C.M. HARTLEY
    1968   J. BLAKEY
    1971   J. BLAKEY
    1992   R. HEUFF
    2001   R. LEACH

(d) Villa. Stucco over brick. Concealed roof. Two storey. Corner pilasters and central architrave with two pairs of Doric pilasters each side of window. Ground floor windows cornices on console brackets

(f) Copper beech 150 year old felled 2007, formal replacement layout: axial path and lawns

(g) HEUFF graphic artist specializing in motor-racing illustration

(a) *(LL)* **22,** THE PINES (1880) MERTON LODGE (1843)

(b) circa 1835 J. SEIR owner

(c) 1843   Miss E. PALMER
1848   Colonel BURROUGHS
1850   Ms A. ELRINGTON
1856   Captain PECHELL
1858   Misses GARNETT
1865   Mrs R. SEIR, owner, Mrs T. ROPER
1873   Revd W. HUME-ROTHERY
1881** Mrs M. ROTHERY, son Joseph and three servants
1895   Mrs LAWSON
1889   J.H. HUME-ROTHERY
1898   Colonel TAYLOR
1899   Mrs A. BLAKISTON
1919   Major N.P. BROOKE £950
1929   Mrs BROOKE
1933   Brigadier General F.B. JOHNSTONE DSO
1944   Miss E.K. BAYLISS £1,300
1944   Ms S.F.L. CARTER £1,500
1949   Miss BAYLISS £1,500
1950   S. OWENS £2,450, then to V. COLLIER architect £3,250
1957   Miss F.N. HASTINGS £3,000, who sold the land on the south side to
H.A. CRAWFORD
1961   Seven flats then converted

(d) Villa. Stucco on brick. Two storeys with basement and attic. Central breakforward.

Centre porch Doric fluted columns. Entablature triglyphs and metopes. Corner pilasters. Extension to south gabled west

(f) Fir. Three Scots pine felled 2004. Prunus. Hawthorne felled in 2005

(f) gate piers

(g) MRS M.C.H. ROTHERY a prominent supporter of Josephine Butler's Ladies National Association and husband William became its president; her father was Joseph Hume MP

W.H. ROTHERY son 1899-1968 educated Cheltenham College and Magdalen College Oxford, RMA Woolwich, became deaf in 1917; First Wolfson Professor of Metallurgy, Oxford. FRS 1937 OBE 1951

(a) *(SL)* **23,** MONA VILLA (1883), TIVOLI COTTAGE (1851), TIVOLI COTTAGE (1838)

(b) circa 1835

(c) 1937   Mrs TATHAM

1844	Miss MATTHEWS
1845	Mr HOLT
1846	Mrs C. HOLT
1859	Mrs E. CHAMBERS
1861	Miss OTWAY, Ms L. BENNETT
1863	Mrs E. CHAMBERS
1864	Miss ASHWIN
1865	Mrs EDWARDS
1876	C. KING retired corn merchant
1882	Captain P. WATTS
1883	H. BERKELEY
1891	Mrs M. NIXON
1910	Mrs FOLEY
1929	Mrs PENN
1930	W. DUDLEY
1933	Misses and Mrs H. M. LEAVEY
1938	Mrs M. UHDE £750
1977	R. REEVES

(d) A pair of semi-detached villas with no 25 much added to and altered. Stucco over brick. Two storey and single storey north. Doric pilasters indicating original façade

(f) Fine cedar of Lebanon which was blown down in 1991, replaced by amber maple, sycamore

---

(a) **24, TIVOLI PLACE**

(b) 1993

(d) Block of eight flats. Four storey. Symmetrical façade with false porch under breakforward. Hipped roof. Windows on the first floor have minimal balconies.

(g) Beech felled 2005

(a) *(SL)* **25, CLEVELAND (1895), HERBERT LODGE (1879), TIVOLI COTTAGE (1847)**

(b) circa 1835

(c)
1844	G.G. PAINE
1861	G. CHAMBERLAIN
1865	S.W. FISHER
1871	Mrs E. SKIPTON
1871	H. BAILEY
1876	R. EDWARDS
1879	Mrs H. KLUGH widow
1891	H. KLUGH

1894 A. RICHARDSON
1907 C. TILLARD
1910 P.E. BODDINGTON
1913 Mrs A. BROWNETT
1929 E. NOTON
1933 Misses NEWMAN
1945 N.J. BISHOP
1955 W.F. LEACH
1983 D. OGDEN developer; re-furbished
1986 I. MORGAN, £107,000
2006 N. DAVIES

(d) pair with no 23 (which see)

(g) RICHARDSON moved 1900 to no 11, where actor son Ralph was born

MORGAN sales and marketing director for a furniture company

(a) **26, LONGFORD COURT** (1960)

(b) 1960

(c) 1961 Sir R.B. WATERER CB, JP, Miss M. WIGGINS, J.S. FOOTE,
        Mrs C. PRITCHARD-EVANS, D.J GREEN, Miss COSKERY

    1968 Mrs P. CRAWFORD, Miss M.E. HOOPER, J.S.K FOOTE, Miss F.R. BURRIDGE,
        D.J. GREEN, Mrs M.A. COSKERY

    1975 Mrs M.A. COSKERY, M.E. HOOPER, M.K. FOOTE, Miss F.R. BURRIDGE,
        D.J. GREEN, M.E. MACKENZIE

    1999* Mrs M. COSKERY, Miss I. STEWART, Mrs E. HAWKINS, D.J. GREEN,
        Ms M. MCKENZIE

(d) Built in the grounds of Longford House, The Park. Three storeys. Rendered.

Ridge roof. Centre entrance and stairs.

(f) Magnolia

(g) WATERER, civil servant

GREEN authority on Morris stained glass

(a) *(SL)* **27,** WHITEHAYES (1910), HERBERT COTTAGE (1858), HERBERT LODGE (1881),
    1 TIVOLIAN VILLAS (1871), TIVOLIA VILLA (1851), TIVOLIAN VILLA 1 (1847)

(b) Circa 1834-40

(c) 1841 W. FRASER

1846   J. CAMPS
1851** Ms A. SMITH charwoman
1858   Mr WHITFIELD
1859   Mrs LAWSON
1859   Mrs LAWSON
1862   Miss PARKINSON
1891   Ms E. AYLIFFE
1893   Mrs ASH
1897   F. HOLMES
1898   G. WILLIAMS
1901   Mrs L. PERREIRA
1910   Miss SADLER
1933   E.C. NOTON
1942   Mrs NOTON
1950   W.E. SEAGRAVE
1961   O.J. SEAGRAVE
1975   D.J. SEAGRAVE
1984   M. OLIVER antiques dealer
1998   N. RATCLIFFE

(d) A pair of semi-detached villas with no. 29. Stucco over brick. Hipped roof. Two storeys. Centre breakforward. Corner Doric pilasters. Horizontal rustication. Windows voussoirs and segmental recesses. End entrances. Doric pilasters.

(f) Cherry tree

(g) RATCLIFFE a Director of Zurich Financial Services Group

(a) *(SL)* **29,** WOODSIDE (1910), 2 TIVOLIAN VILLAS (1871), HERBERT VILLA (1853), TIVOLIA VILLA 2 (1851), TIVOLIAN VILLAS 2 (1847)

(b) 1843

(c) 1843   Captain GUY
1844   Miss GUY
1847   Mrs E. DOWSE
1858   Mrs E. READ
1861   Mrs MOCKLER
1862   Mrs EDMONDS
1863   J.W. BRADSHAW
1865   J. PARKINSON, owner
1871   G. BURY

1874   Miss BAILLIE
1881   T. PIFF carpenter and joiner
1881   Miss S. BUCKLE
1894   Miss WYNN-ROBERTS
1899   Mile MONTET
1901   H. POTTER
1910   H. ROGERS
1929   Mrs YALDWYN
1932   Mrs J. ELLIS, Misses MURTON
1935   S.J. CLARKE
1962   M. KIRBY, M. PRESCOTT
1994   P. CLARKE £225,000
2004   D. HARRISON architect

(d) As for number 27

(f) Hawthorne

Bottle-well beside portway lane on west. Iron gates replicas, installed by Kirby.

(g) S. CLARKE was Borough Librarian

KIRBY was director of Marshalls Ironmasters

P. CLARKE was managing director of oil service company, Aberdeen

---

(a) **31** WHITECROFT (1931)

(b) 1931   J. CHESTERS to R.V. COPELAND

(c) 1936   G.G. MARSLAND BSc
     1942   E.M. DENISON
     1980   G. LISTER

(d) Idiom suburban Norman Shaw. Brick. Two storeys. Centre gable over entrance.

(f) Monterey cypress felled 1997 replaced by honey lotus, fir, prunus

(g) MARSLAND became Town Clerk

(a) **FIRS COURT HOTEL**, (1936), RAVENSCOURT (1898), ST EDMUNDS (1839)

(b) 1838   T.H. BENNET, builder, to W. EVANS

(c) 1839   Colonel C.B. EVANS
   1844   Mrs B. COOKE
   1854   Captain C. STURT
   1862   Mrs GARRETT
   1865   Colonel IMPEY
   1866   Lady THOMPSON
   1868   Lieutenant Colonel G. WATSON
   1873   Revd E. CORNFORD
   1879   C.P.A. OMAN
   1882   Mrs A. OMAN widow
   1886   R. DENNIS
   1898   Colonel C. GARBETT
   1899   Deputy Surgeon
          General CLIFTON
   1901   Colonel B. BENNETT
   1929   F. JOYNER
   1933   J. CHESTERS
   1936   T. SHANLEY
   1950   Major D.J. DONALD, F. ELLIOT, Miss PRATT, L. HILL-TOOT
   1957   E.H. TAYLOR
   1963   D. PULLEN
   1968   A. LIVINGSTONE
   1971   N.A. ALLEN, R.F. EMERY, P. MILNE, Q.A. MATHESON
   1972   WEST COUNTRY BREWERIES LTD TO WESTERN ESTATES
   1973   ALLEN, MATHESON
   1974   GLYNBRIDGE BUILDING AND DEVELOPMENT LTD to W. BAYSTON
   Demolished

(g) STURT explorer of Australia, intended knighthood but died before accolade. Widow lived at S. Johns Lodge, Tivoli Circus

OMAN'S son, Charles (1860-1946) was at Oxford, historian especially of Peninsular War, and the Middle Ages; Chichele Professor of history at Oxford and MP for University 1919-35; grand-daughter Julia married Sir Roy Strong, died 2003. Previously OMAN had lived at 5 Park Place

BAYSTON of CASTLE GODWYN, Painswick

(h) 1952 Two hotel residents robbed Cavendish House department store, leaving a toe print on broken glass, resulting in the first conviction through this type of evidence.

(a) **TIVOLI COURT** on site of FIRS COURT HOTEL

(b) 1974

(c) 1975   G.C. BLOOM (1)
1977   W. WALDRON (2)
1976   BRENNAN dentist (3)
1977   J. HILL (3)
1992   Miss J. TROTTER (1)
2007   M. WALDRON (2)

(d) Terrace of three neo-Georgian houses. Porches have Doric columns under pediments. Concealed roof.

(f) Fir, maple

(g) BLOOM joined Reuters after Oxford , opening bureaux in Manilla, Shanghai, Mexico City, Buenos Aires. Later in London with Press Association. CBE 1974

W. WALDRON bomber pilot RAFVR. Staff College; War Cabinet Office; India with Lord Mountbatten; Ministry of Aviation, opening post-war airline routes in Far East, South Africa and Caribbean, 1966 General Manager Heathrow Airport

TROTTER Principal of Cheltenham and Gloucester College of Higher Education then first Vice-Chancellor of University of Gloucestershire, DBE. Lord-Lieutenant of Gloucestershire, 2010.

(a) **33a,** 35a (1957)

(b) 1928-53: conversion from stabling and d/garage with artist studio above for Mrs MASCIE-TAYLOR; converted to a dwelling comprising living room, study and cloakroom. Art nouveau weather boarding to east gable. South entrance set back, 1955 architect FODEN, ARIBA

(c) 1953   Mrs M. HUTTON
1955   Mrs B.E. JUCKES
1960   G.G. DENT £4,200
1975   Mrs M. E. DENT
1987   A. SAMPSON £71,950

(d) 1988 north light replaced by tiles.

Study opened into living room 1987

(f) Garden divided from no 35's; fine copper beech

(g) SAMPSON author, artist and local historian; wife professional violinist

(a) *(SL)* **35,** KEMERTON, KEMERTON COURT (1961), KEMERTON COURT HOTEL (1955), KEMERTON LODGE (1848) Charlotte Hepton, Parkinson's wife, from Kemerton, Worcestershire, TALAVERA LODGE (1847)

(b) 1841-4

(c)
1844	T. TYERS
1845	R. SMITH
1846	Colonel KIRBY
1847	J. PARKINSON
1860	J. LEA
1871	Mrs F. HOPTON
1881	Mrs C. PARKINSON, widow
1910	Revd P. BURD, Misses ARMSTRONG nieces
1924	J.A. LADE £900
1928	J. MASCIE-TAYLOR £1,650
1957	Mrs M. HUTTON £4,750
1961	S.A. BOND MB, CHB, FRCS
1963	J.R.H. JEENS, H. WYNN
1968	J.R.H. JEENS
1973	J. NESS-WALKER
1979	Sir P. SCARLETT, diplomat
1990	M. PECKITT
2001	N. KIRKPATRICK, eye surgeon

(d) Villa stucco over brick. Two storeys and basement. Ends with Doric pilasters.

Centre porch Doric pilasters. Pediment.

(f) 2001 garden bulldozed leaving only magnolia, strawberry tree, lime and pond

(g) PARKINSON also owned 27 and 29 Tivoli Rd

SCARLETT ambassador to Norway 1955, Vatican 1960; chairman Cathedrals Advisory Committee 1967-81; KCMG 1985, KCVO 1955 (1905-87)

(a) **37,** LESLIE LODGE (1878), THE FERNS/FERN LODGE (1851), ST JAMES VILLA (1847)

(b) 1840   T.H. BENNETT builder

(c)
1843	Revd J. BALFOUR
1845	J. LEECH
1846	Lieutenant Colonel BRAY
1848	Miss M. BIDDULPH
1851	Major J. SCARGILL
1854	Mrs COL. WATTS
1858	Mrs BUCHANAN

1866   Surgeon Major H. BAILLIE
1866   Miss BAILLIE
1871   E. MACKLER
1873   C. WINTOUR
1878   Mrs J. HANDLEY
1895   Colonel C. ELLIS
1910   Colonel R.J. STAINFORTH
1918   W.H. BOND
1942   H. SILVER
1950   J.B. GILLON
1957   Mrs GILLON
1968   R.F. SELLEY
1975   C.W. SPENCER
1985   A. KNIGHTLY-BROWN architect

(d) Pair of semi-detached villas with 39. Two storeys and basement and attics.

End gables breakforwards. Window hood-moulds. Central shared porch, parapet traceried motifs, offset buttresses. Finials to gables. Tudor-gothic idiom

(f)   Alegnus blown down 2006, holm oak, hornbeam, maple, hawthorn

---

(a) **39,** MORFORDS (1980), DRY HOW (1929), THE FERNS (1876), FERN LODGE (1871), PARK LODGE (1847)

(b) 1840   as for no 37

(c) 1846   I. LEECH owner
1847   Mrs M. TATHAM
1849   H. RUDYARD
1851   Honourable MS L. BUTLER
1852   W. PARKER
1856   Baroness WYLEY
1858   Misses BLAND
1861   Ms E. LEECH owner
1862   DAWSON LITTLEDALE
1864   Mrs HOOPER
1868   V.B. WEBB owner
1871   H. NEALE owner
1871   Mrs MOCKLER
1874   Dr. MOCKLER
1876   C. WINTOUR
1878   Mrs DAY
1881   Mrs Colonel J. WATSON widow
1888   A.B. PINCKNEY

1896   Mrs B. GARDNER
1905   Brigadier Surgeon LLOYDS
1929   Miss FLETCHER
1939   Miss M.M. GRAHAM
1942   T.S. COPPLESTONE
1950   Mrs JOHNSTONE
1961   Miss A. JOHNSTONE
1963   A.N. BERESFORD
1975   A.C. WHITEHOUSE
----   ELGOOD
1978   P. BARLOW

(d) As for no. 37

(f) Beech

(g) DAWSON-LITTLEDALE devised lettering in relief for blind. 1838 "Littledale Type"

MOCKLER Inspector General, Army Medical Dept

BERESFORD's sister Elizabeth children's-book writer including "Wombles"

BARLOW solicitor and linguist MBE 2009; wife linguist and local historian

---

(a) **41** PARK LEA (1933), YARROWBY (1897), ALMA VILLA (1861), PARK COTTAGE (1858)

(b) circa 1840

(c) 1843   Mrs CODRINGTON
1846   Mrs REEVES
1847   Mrs TATHAM
1849   Miss PALMER
1851** Miss M. WEDLEY cook
1858   Mrs MOCKLER
1861   J.T. COTTAM
1862   T.R. WILSON
1865   F. HAWLINGS
1867   Mrs WARRINGTON
1868   Mrs GRIFFITHS
1870   T. HOLMES
1876   Misses HOLMES
1879   Revd R. DREAPER
1881** P. BENDAL upholsterer and six children
1887   O. DAVIES
1890   Miss J. DAVIES
1891   A. SHIRER

1897   Miss H. READY, Miss E. HOGGINS
1929   Mrs GATHACOLE
1933   Mrs JOHNSON
1939   G. PARSLOE
1957   I.A. LANE
1971   M.C. MULCAHY, Mrs P. CRAIG
1981   A. HART
2000   P. LEIGHTON

(d) Villa. Stucco over brick. Two storeys and basement. Concealed roof. Central entrance. Ground floor windows under shallow arch recess. Central slight breakforward. No cornice but flattened frieze and corner pilaster, all very basic.

(a)   **41a,** LEA HOUSE on site of TIVOLI GARDENS

(c)   1865   Tivoli Gardens owned by W.N. SKILLICORNE
      1881**   H. MOORMAN, nurseryman, three children and parents. Carpenter, sister dressmaker and son
      1929   Mrs S. MOORMAN
      1930   Miss A. MOORMAN fruit grower
      House built
      1985   Mrs M. MELLERUP
      1995   R. OLSEN typographer

(d)   Villa. Two storeys. Ridge roof. Moulded window surrounds. Centre entrance porch with distyle Doric columns. Intended as companion to no 43. Also set back from road.

(f)   eucalyptus

(a)   **43,** PARK COTTAGE (1847) on site of TIVOLI GARDENS

(b)   1840s

(c)   1933   J.G. HALLIDAY
      1939   Miss HAMMOND
      1942   W. BARNETT
      1963   A. GINDERS
      1989   S. GORDELIER power engineer

(d)   Villa. Stucco over brick. Two storeys. Moulded window surrounds. Concealed roof.

      Central doorway. Architrave with console brackets. Set back from road

(f)   leylandii, cherry

(a) **45**

(b) Mid twentieth century

(c) 1961   Major T.I. HARDIE
    1978   BRIERS
            A. PHILIPS
    1990   Miss I. ARMITAGE

(d) Detached. Two storeys and conspicuous attic conversion

(f) beech, holly

(a) **OLD COACH HOUSE** (2006) ISILINGO (1968)

(b) circa 1833-50 if contemporary with present house 109 The Park

(c) 1968   A.H. DAVIS
    1975   Mrs DAVIS
    2006   M. BLANCHFIELD

(d) Coach house for 107 and 109 The Park. Semi-detached with 105 The Park.

Extended in 2006 by the north wing

ST. STEPHENS ROAD

ITS LOCATION WAS determined by the boundary of Cox's Orchard on the west and Westall Fairlong on the east and its name variously given as 'the road leading to the Zoological Gardens', 'Hatherley Place' and, finally, 'St. Stephen's Road' when the church was consecrated in 1883. This thoroughfare has, since 1834, been dominated at its northern end by the impressive terrace of Hatherley Place. Complemented at the southern end by Parkgate and Redesdale, together with the substantial presence of St. Stephen's Manor, and punctuated by the church midway, this streetscape of largely 19th and 20th century houses offers an agreeable variety of styles.

Until 1870 when the road was made officially a public highway, maintenance was the responsibility of private owners. Petitions to the authorities led by R. S. Lingwood of Redesdale in 1857 and 1864 were unsuccessful, primarily because of inadequate surfacing; but worse was to follow even after adoption, when the drainage and sewers raised health concerns. It was not until 1911 that new pipes were laid, and even these had to be replaced in 1938 because rats had gnawed through them! With such hazardous roads and pavements, street lighting too was a necessity, and again Lingwood persuaded the Town Commissioners to provide it.

Lingwood was but one of the many persons associated with this road who played leading roles in Cheltenham's history: residents or landlords like Winterbotham, Captain and Lady Henry and, of course, Pearson Thompson.

(a) *(SL)* **HATHERLEY PLACE**

(b) 1834-40 at least 5 of the 13 houses built for PEARSON THOMPSON of Hatherley Court

(c) See individual houses

(d) Three storeys and basement. Double front with doorway varying in position. Continuous first floor balcony with bowed rods and frieze of circles. Individual balconies to second floor of 22 and 24. Change of roof line at 18 suggests stages of building, with 26 showing a third stage.

(f) At rear brick walled courtyard, garages converted from stables. Access to INKERMAN LANE, till late 1990s Hatherley Place Lane.

(a) *(SL)* **2**, (1939) 1, HATHERLEY PLACE

(b) See group entry

(c)
1841	R. BISHOP, Miss GOULD
1850	L.H. GRAY, Mrs Captain ELLIS
1855	Miss WHEATLEY
1860	Mrs RAVENSHAW
1865	Mrs STYLES
1870	M. PRINGLE
1875	Mrs BRAY
1880	Mrs MANLEY
1895	Miss MESSENGER
1910	G. PHILLIPS
1916	Mrs WEST, Mrs L. TAYLOR, Mrs WOLFE, Mrs BENDY
1921	G. STEVENS
1925	S. STEPHENS
1930	S. STEPHENS, Miss L. LAURD, Mrs SAVERY
1939	S. STEPHENS
1968	N. PREECE, M. GODWIN
1973	P. WHITTLE
1999*	G. COLE (1) Ms C. HEATHCOTE (3) Mrs J. DELL, P. SMITH (4)

(d) (e) (f) (g) (h) See group entry

(a) *(SL)* **4**, (1939) 2, HATHERLEY PLACE

(b) See group entry

(c) 1837   Mrs General JACKSON
    1841   Mrs DALRYMPLE
    1850   B. WICHCOTE
    1855   Mrs BENNETT
    1860   E. TANNER, Mrs MONY
    1865   E. TANNER, Captain MORANT
    1870   Captain MORANT
    1880   Revd PARGETER
    1885   J. KNIGHT
    1900   Mr FERGUSON
    1910   J. WINTLE
    1939   Mrs STRACHAN
    1950   Mrs STRACHAN, F. MIDGLEY
    1957   Mrs STRACHAN, N. GRIFFITHS
    1963   T. ROSS
    1968   M. O'BRIAN
    1973   J. BECK
    1999*   P. JENNINGS

(d) (e) (f) (g) (h) See group entry

(a) *(SL)* **6,** (1939) BRYN - IVOR (1920) 3, HATHERLEY PLACE

(b) See group entry

(c) 1837   Revd C. HERBERT
    1841   Miss BEAUCHAMP
    1865   Revd A. REEKE
    1870   T. SANDERSON
    1880   Mrs HUGHES
    1889   Lieutenant Colonel WILLIAMSON
    1900   Mrs WILLIAMSON
    1905   Mrs GREENWOOD
    1910   E. WOOD
    1921   Mrs L. MUNDAY
    1926   F. CLIFFORD
    1939   Mrs CLIFFORD
    1957   Miss HENRY, Mrs TOLHURST
    1963   Mrs H. HARVEY, Mrs TOLHURST
    1968   Mrs TOLHURST, Miss V. RUTLAND

1973   Miss RUTLAND

1999*   Ms C. MUDDIMAN (1) Ms P. MARSTON (3) Ms N. SIMPSON, A. WHITE (4)
        R. THOMAS (5)

(d) See group entry

(e) 1844 a lodging house

(f) (g) (h) See group entry

(a) *(SL)* **8,** (1939) 4, HATHERLEY PLACE

(b) See group entry

(c) 1841   Miss PRICE
     1850   C. BEALE
     1855   Mrs PYECROFT
     1860   Miss PYECROFT
     1875   Mrs SKIPTON
     1880   Mrs TARLTON
     1890   Mrs TARLTON
     1895   W. DAVIES
     1900   Mr JANES
     1905   J. WINTLE
     1921   C. HAWARD
     1926   W. BARBER, D. STEEL
     1935   A. MEREATE, Mrs F. WOODIN, F. TIESOC
     1939   Mrs C. BACKER
     1950   R. GABBOTT
     1957   B. BELCHER
     1968   B. BELCHER, P. BREWER, D. DOWDING
     1973   D. DOWDING
     1999*   Ms P. STRONACH (garden flat) D. DOWDING (ground floor)
             J. SKINNER (maisonette)

(d) (e) (f) (g) (h) See group entry

(a) *(SL)* **10,** (1939), 5 HATHERLEY PLACE

(b) See group entry

(c) 1841   Mrs BLACKWOOD
     1850   Miss CURRY
     1855   Misses CURRY
     1880   Misses BUBB
     1895   G. SCHNEIDER

1905   Mrs SCHNEIDER

1921   Miss A. SCHNEIDER

1930   Misses SCHNEIDER

1950   Miss SCHNEIDER

1963   P. O'HANLON

1968   Mrs E. O'HANLON

1973   E. HURST

1999*   F. PAXTON (ground floor) S. BROWN (first floor) W. MARFELL, Ms J. TELLANDER (top flat)

(d) (e) (f) (g) (h) See group entry

(a) *(SL)* **12,** (1939) 6, HATHERLEY PLACE

(b) See group entry

(c) 1841   D. CURLING

1850   Miss WATERS

1855   Captain FULLERTON

1860   Mrs GIBBINGS

1880   Mrs GREEN

1895   Major General FRANCIS

1900   Miss MESSENGER

1916   Mrs A. LUMSDAINE

1921   Mrs DORIA, Mrs CREESE

1926   Fr PLENTY, Fr TURNER

1930   S. RUSSELL, W. JONES

1935   Miss G. BROWNING

1950   Miss M. MAUDE, Miss V. RICHINGS

1963   Miss MAUDE, H. WOODWARD

1968   P. HOLLARD, H. WOODWARD

1973   H. WOODWARD, M. DARWELL

1999*   Ms C. PEARCE (basement) S. SMILES (3) A. RAWLINGS (4)

(d) (e) (f) (g) (h) See group entry

(a) *(SL)* **14,** (1939) STANMORE (1905) 7, HATHERLEY PLACE

(b) See group entry

(c) 1841   W. HILL

1850   Captain B. JORDON

1855   Mrs MONRO

1880   T. HUGHES

1895   Mrs SWINEY

1905   Mrs E. HOSKINS
1916   F. JELFS, W. NICHOLS, H. WOTTON
1921   F. JELFS, upholsterer
1942   Mrs A. JELFS
1957   Mrs EKSTELIS
1968   H. DEITZER
1973   C. BRYDSON
1999*   T. WHALES (ground floor) J. THOMAS (studio) Ms D. GREEN (3)
        Ms S. RUDGE (4)

(d) (e) (f) (g) (h) See group entry

(a)   *(SL)* **16,** (1939) ROSSLEIGH (1920) HAMPDEN (1905) 8, HATHERLEY PLACE

(b)   See group entry

(c)   1841   J. CAMPBELL
      1850   Mrs GRAHAME
      1855   Hon Mrs PERY
      1865   Mrs MONEY
      1875   Mrs GIBBINGS
      1880   Miss SHAW, Mrs HOUGHTON
      1885   Miss SHAW
      1890   Miss SHAW, Mrs BELL
      1900   Mrs GORDON, Mrs R. ANDERSON
      1905   Commander BEAUCHAMP RN
      1921   Mrs A. FRYS
      1926   Misses HANDCOCK
      1935   F. ASHWIN
      1963   E. HARRIS
      1999*   D. EDMISTON, Ms P. TODD

(d)   See group entry

(e)   Guest house (1942), apartments (1935)

(f) (g) (h) See group entry

(a)   *(SL)* **18,** (1939) 9, HATHERLEY PLACE

(b)   See group entry

(c)   1841   G. GORDON
      1850   Mrs MORRIS
      1855   Mrs PHAYRE
      1865   R. CHAMBERLAIN
      1870   Mrs BOODLE

1875   Revd A. STERT
1880   Mrs STERT
1895   Revd E. JENNINGS
1900   Captain H. ROCHFORT RN
1921   Mrs BURTON
1926   J. HANCHET
1968   P. JOHNSON
1973   I. DRYLAND
1999*   C. LANGDON

(d) See group entry

(e) Apartments (1926)

(f) (g) (h) See group entry

(a) *(SL)* **20,** (1939) 10, HATHERLEY PLACE

(b) See group entry

(c) 1841   Revd H. GRIFFITHS
     1855   Mrs EDEN
     1860   Mrs NUGENT
     1865   Mrs DE LAUTOUR
     1870   Mrs G. HARRISON
     1875   Mrs HARRISON, Miss NICHOLLS
     1880   Dr CARR
     1921   Mrs G. DOUGLAS
     1926   Mrs BARTON
     1930   Miss C. JONES MD, J. JONES
     1939   J. ANDREWS
     1950   Mrs C. MATHEWS
     1963   G. DIXON
     1999*   R. ALLEN, G. DOE (1) Ms R. PFLEGER (2) J. WEST (3)

(d) (e) (f) See group entry

(g) GRIFFITHS educated Rugby, active in Cheltenham Cricket and Rugby Clubs, died aged 85 in 1892.

(h) See group entry

(a) *(SL)* **22,** (1939) 11, HATHERLEY PLACE

(b) See group entry

(c) 1841   H. SEYMOUR, Lady WHITCOMB
     1850   Revd A. BOYD

1855   Major SAVORY
1860   Mrs DALZELL
1865   Lieutenant Colonel MCCALLUM
1885   Miss CHAMBERLAYNE
1890   Deputy Surgeon General CARR
1910   Mrs C. CARR
1926   Mrs CLARKE, E. BAINTON
1930   E. BAINTON, Revd R. BOULTER, R.G. DANSAGE
1935   F. GOSLING
1957   Mrs WILLSON, G. DIXON
1963   M. DARBYSHIRE
1968   W. SUGG
1973   P. SUGG
1999* N. JACOBS, Ms C. WRIGHT (1) J. MCDONNELL (2) Ms K. AKRILL (4)
       D. MANDERS, Ms D. CANTRILL (5) S. PARKER (6) Ms G. CRAWLEY (7)

(d) (e) (f) See group entry

(g) BOYD vicar of Christ Church, founder of parish school 1847; Canon of Gloucester Cathedral 1857, Dean of Exeter 1867, died 1884.

(h) See group entry.

(a) *(SL)* **24,** (1939), 12, HATHERLEY PLACE

(b) See group entry

(c) 1841   Mrs HORNE
    1850   Mrs DALZELL
    1860   C. TENNANT
    1875   Mrs E. ROWLEY
    1895   Miss E. JONES
    1900   Miss ASH, Miss FIGG
    1905   Revd E. JENNINGS
    1916   Misses D'ARGENT, Miss AITKIN, Miss MACLEOD
    1926   F. COURT, Miss B. TAYLOR, C. GIBBS, Miss EDWARDS
    1930   Miss B. TAYLOR, T. DIPPER, Miss EDWARDS, Mrs H. TOLHURST
    1935   Miss TAYLOR, Mrs MAISEY, Mrs L. BOYD-CARPENTER, Mrs TOLHURST
    1963   G. ETTLE, Miss TAYLOR
    1968   Miss TAYLOR
    1999* Ms C. LEVITT (1A) J. SPENCER (1B) J. GARNER (2) M. SAXTON (3)
         Ms A. BUTLER (4) R. THOMAS (5) P. COWIN (6) Ms J. DARBYSHIRE (7)

(d) See group entry

(e) 1895 Preparatory School for boys

(f) (g) (h) See group entry.

(a) **REGENT COURT** (1975), HILTON LODGE (1970s), NUBIE HOUSE (1855)

(b) circa 1850-1975; then Regent Court custom-built 40 flats. After 1895 postal address was Lansdown Road

(c) 1855   H. BURGH
    1875   E. MEYRICKE

(d) Two storeyed. Central roof attic. Three bays, two-storey and extension for picture gallery by J. MIDDLETON late 1860s

(f) 1861 two aspen trees on path felled *"forest days of bygone generation"*

(g) MEYRICKE'S three sons died tragically: Robert in Boer war 1900, twin in steeplechase 1905, Rupert 1916 of blood poisoning in Malta

(h) Auction 1869 of house contents, including paintings from gallery of Flemish and Italian schools; 170 lots raised £16-17,000

(a) **HANOVER HOUSE** (1970), BAYSHILL NURSING HOME (1957), DEVON HOUSE (1925), SMEATON HOUSE (1903), QUINCE LAWN (1889), HATHERLEY VILLA (1854)

(b) circa 1850 including 2 cottages till 2004

(c) 1854   Captain HENRY

    1865   Lady SELINA HENRY
    1870   Misses HENRY
    1890   H. MCCOLL
    1903   P. KENWORTHY
    1916   W. BANKIER
    1921   P. KENWORTHY
    1926   A. DRAKE
    1933   Mrs DRAKE
    1936   Mrs DRAKE, Devon House Cottages, R. ROSS, G. TATUM
    1942   Mrs DRAKE, F. JENKINS, G. TATUM
    1957   Miss H. CASSUM matron; T. HARRIS, A. BLACKMORE
    1967   HANOVER HOUSING ASSOCIATION, 40 apartments

(d) Original frontage plain with stone porch. Two storeys. Gables south-east and north-east corners. 1889 sale lists five reception, thirteen bedroom, minton-tiled floor in portico entrance.

(e) Private apartments for retired, 1967

(f) "Carriage drive, lawns south and west, ornate fountain; 3 glasshouses, paddock, stables, double coach house, harness room, laundry" - 1889 sale description

Sale 1890 stated 3 reception rooms, 10 bedrooms and grounds, 2 rockeries, vegetable and fruit gardens, 2 cottages which were in south-west corner of site now occupied by PEGASUS COURT.

(g) LADY SELINA HENRY was third surviving daughter of first Marquis of Hastings and Countess of Loudon, died 1867 and at her request buried with her maid servant in Bouncers Lane cemetery, Prestbury. It is probable that she had ancestral links with Selina, Countess of Huntingdon who married Theophilus Hastings, ninth Earl of Huntingdon in 1728 and who founded chapels denoted as the Countess of Huntingdon's Connexion – one being in North Place, Cheltenham.

(a) **21,** FAIRLIGHT, 2 (1930-3), PENSHURST (1921)

(b) Mid nineteenth century

(c) 1865   Mr ELLIOTT
     1880   Miss SHITTLER
     1895   Miss SINGER
     1900   T. POWELL
     1916   W. SURFLEET
     1921   C. PARSONS
     1930   Mrs B. JACKSON
     1942   Mrs B. JACKSON, Ms M. NEATE photographer
     1950   Mrs E. CHESTER
     1975   H. THOMAS, P. HANNAFORD
     1999* J. SKILLMAN

(d) Upper windows decorated stone mouldings

(g) ELLIOTT having unsuccessfully requested road to be adopted by Commissioners had his costs paid by Bubb & Co 1865

(a) **22, PEGASUS COURT**

(b) circa 1980's

     49 apartments for retired persons with conservatory, laundry, 2 guest suites.

(d) Pair of neo-Georgian 4 storey blocks linked by glazed communal room rendered with rusticated ground floor each having porch distyle and staircase window through first and second floors, wide eaves. Behind rendered concave 2 storey range surmounted by clock tower centre, at end extremity brick pairs of apartments.

(f) Communal garden with raised beds and centre pool and fountain.

(a) **23, RATHLIN** (2000) SHERWOOD

(b) circa 1890

(c) 1890   Revd C. DOUTON
     1900   Mrs P. DICKSON
     1910   Miss SWEET-ESCOTT
     1921   F. HUSSEY
     1961   F. WATSON, Mrs C. ROBERTS
     1968   F. WATSON, G. REESON
     1973   F. WATSON
     1999*   Ms J. WATSON (ground floor) Ms J. CARROLL (the flat)

(d) Bay each side of central door where arch with keystone and decorated finial stops. Decorative string course below first floor windows

(f) 1923 map shows the house extends over two plots between 21 and 25. One original stone gate pier

(g) DOUTON was the curate of St. Stephen's from 1891 to 1892

(a) *(LL)* **25, WALTON HOUSE,** (1990s), ST. STEPHEN'S VICARAGE (1942), TREHALE (1930s), No. 34 (1905), THE LAURELS (1875)

(b) circa 1875

(c) 1875   Mrs PAINE
     1880   Miss TRISTRAM
     1885   Miss W. PAGAN, Miss LONSDALE
     1895   J. MEREDITH
     1905   Mrs FORSYTH
     1921   Miss FORSYTH-GRANT
     1927   Captain J. FORSYTH-GRANT
     1933   Misses JONES
     1942   Revd G. HILDER MA
     1950   Revd A. SAINT MA
     1961   Revd G. WILLIS BVSc
     1968   Major D. INLAY
     1975   R. PENTYCROSS
     1999*   N. FORBES-GEORGE

(d) Stucco, 2 storey, 1 storey entrance by stone steps and porch, 5 light fanlight, windows classical surround

(f) 3 original gate piers with gates circa 2000

(a) *(LL)* **26,** HATHERLEY GRANGE RESIDENTIAL HOME (1968), HATHERLEY GRANGE (1895), 13, HATHERLEY PLACE

(b) See group entry

(c) 1841   Mrs Colonel READ, Mrs KERSHAW
    1844   A. CROFT
    1855   Mrs TIMMINS
    1860   Mrs MCKENZIE
    1880   Revd J. SHULDHAM
    1895   A. LITHGOW
    1921   Mrs F. TURNER
    1926   A. SIMS
    1942   R. WHITE
    1950   G. WILLIAMS, D. GOBLE, A. CARR,
             H. COOKSEY MBE
    1957   G. WILLIAMS, K. OLIVER, W. WALSH
    1963   Mrs C. ANDREWS, G. WILLIAMS, J. BROTHERTON, Mrs COOK
    1968   S. IDDLES, I. TRACEY

(d) See group entry

(e) Residential Home, 1968

(f) See group entry

(g) CROFT and wife members of 'fashionable Enterpean Society', hosting in their drawing room morning concerts when amateurs like 'Cianchetini, Uglow, Evans, Col Wall and Dr Boisragon performed in a Haydn Quartet.'

OLIVER RWS, ARE head of printmaking at College of Art and Design.

(h) See group entry

(a) **27, CODENHAM LODGE** on site of villa

(b) C. WINSTONE builder

(c) 1876   F. LONGE
    1900   Col W. LEIR JP
    1905   Mrs GRIMLEY
    1921   Miss E. HILL
    1927   Mrs OLSON, Mrs V. ENNIS
    1961   Mrs OLSON, Mrs V. ENNIS, Mrs E. CLARKE
    1968   J. O'KELLY, Mrs V. ENNIS
    1973   W. MADDOCKS

(d) Demolished, four storey block of six flats

(g) LONGE one of the petitioners for renaming 'St. Stephen's Road'

(a) **29, THE COPPERS** (1965)

(b) 1965

(c) 1968   W. MYATT

(d) 2000   much extended

(f) On land originally Hatherley Lodge's. Original gate piers from Hatherley Lodge.

Wall evidence iron railings

(a) **29A,** (1965) HATHERLEY LODGE, 29, (1885)

(b) circa 1885

(c) 1885   Major G. STEPHENS
    1905   Mrs G. STEPHENS
    1910   T. DE WINTON
    1936   Lieutenant Colonel H. LEAPMAN
    1939   C. PERMAN
    1957   Captain K. JAMES
    1968   V. MOODY
    1973   J. FENEMORE
    1999*   Z. EALAND (flat 1) H. NIGHTINGALE (3)

(d) Square villa, one bay, stone porch, basement. Mirror of 33 Thruxton

---

(a) **28** and **30**
    32 and **34** / **28** and **30** (1957)

    36 and **38**
    32a and **32b** (1961)

(b) Built on gardens for tenants of Hatherley Place, in stages:
    28 and 30 in 1968, 36 and 38 in 1961, 32 and 34 in 1957
    Land owned by J. Winterbotham, solicitor

(c) 1957   L. WEAVER (28) J. LANE (30)
    1961   L. WEAVER (28) Mrs E. MARTIN (30) D. KING (32a) E. WILKINSON (32b)
    1968   S. COTTRELL (28) Mrs WEB (30) L. WEAVER (32)
    1973   E. HOLDER (28) Mrs WEBB (30) Miss A. SCHUSTER (32)
    1999*   G. MOXON (no. 28) WEBB (30) SCHUSTER (32) JONES (34) J. DUFFY (36)
            Mrs M. REES (38)

(d) Three pairs of two storey semi-detached houses, rendered. 28, 30, 32 and 40 have centre bays full height; 36 and 38 have ground level only bays: 28 and 30 have front doors; 32 and 34 have side doors; 36 and 38 have front doors under open porch, roof extending over bay windows.

(f) SCHUSTER was the great granddaughter of Cameron Bruce-Pryce who bought Westholme, Overton Road, from architect Middleton 1884. She gave a description of the house to Bowes Museum where fittings from it are kept. Her father, Lieutenant Colonel L. Schuster DSO, was at the siege of Ladysmith, and his cousin lived at Heysham House, Park Place

---

(a) **31,** THE OLD COACH HOUSE of Hatherley Lodge

(b) circa 1865

(c) 1942 F. BUTLER
    1950 P. KAY
    1957 R. WALKER
    1968 N. BAILEY
    1999* J. ORCHARD

(d) Symmetrical three bay. Centre door

(f) Iron railings. Two original stone piers

(a) **33,** THRUXTON from Thruxton Manor, Hampshire ancestral homes of NOYES

(b) circa 1883 C. WINSTONE

(c) 1884 D. NOYES £2,000 from manor of Cheltenham annual rent 1gn
    1927 Mrs SWINHOE at auction £1,750
    1927 Mrs M. KNOLLYS £1,600
    1933 Mrs E. TAPSFIELD
    1949 N. HORTON MBE £5,250
    1961 Major J. CRAWFORD £5,200

(d) Stucco. Two floors. ½ basement. Mirror of Hatherley Lodge

(e) conversion to 8 flats

(f) Part of the site was sold in 1961 to R.W. TAPSELL builder for 35

(g) NOYES from Thruxton: public works in India; mother bought Redesdale in The Park 1878; brother Col. Noyes lived at Parkfield Lawn

TAPSFIELD wife of G. Tapsfield MA the Associate Master of Cheltenham College

HORTON Transport Manager

(a) **35,** TRITON HOUSE, RANMORE

(b) circa 1965

(c) 1961 R.W. TAPSELL builder acquired land part of no 33

1968   R. TAPSELL
1973   M. SIMPSON
1999* D. EDWARDS

(d) Three bay. Two storey. Large garage projects in front of house giving covered area across front of house

---

(a) **40,** (1968) PRINCES COURT (2007) 34 (1939) FALLOWFIELD (1887) ST STEPHEN'S GRANGE (1886)

(b) 1886

(c) 1887   H. JAMES MA
    1897   Revd E. JENNINGS
    1905   Misses BUCHANAN-KER
    1921   Mrs G. WITTS
    1930   A. PRUEN solicitor
    1950   Mrs G. RESTELL-LITTLE
    1957   J. CREW, S. RATCLIFFE
    1961   Mrs E. HUMPHREY
    1968   D. ROBERTS, L. TAYLOR
    c1980 conversion to flats

(d) Stucco. Two floors. Wide eaves on console brackets. Main entrance on Princes Rd. Walled steps. Stone porch. Bay.

(e) 1887 A cramming school was held daily from 4-5:30, "vacation classes" arithmetic, Euclid, algebra

    1897 St Stephen's vicarage

(f) gate piers

(g) JAMES had moved from Hillcourt, Marle Hill

(h) 1897 Queen Victoria's Jubilee celebration in the vicarage "rooms hung with flags of all colours, bust of the Queen... every member of the Mothers' Union received a Jubilee brooch"

(a) *(SL)* **ST. STEPHEN'S CHURCH** choice of dedication by vicar of Christchurch

(b) chancel 1873; nave aisles, north-west porch 1885; south porch, south transept 1888; lady chapel 1920. J. Middleton and L. Barnard.

    Gothic Decorated style. Chancel £1,000; nave £3,395

(c) incumbents:
    1884   C. MCARTHUR
    1891   E. JENNINGS

1915   F. GOODWYN
1917   R. HODSON
1926   A. ADDENBROOKE
1936   R. SUTCH
1941   G. HILDER
1948   A. SAINT
1960   G. WILLIS
1964   F. CROSS
1972   J. GOTT
1989   J. HEIDT
1995   I. BURBERRY
1999   P. NAYLOR

(d) Interior polychromatic stonework. West end rich carving of Apostles above blind arcade, east end statues of King Alfred and Queen Victoria, iron chancel screen 1897, hanging Rood 1945 stained glass Heaton Butler and Bayne. Curtis Ward and Hughes Font 1880. Exterior railings and gates

(e) South transept was converted for partial social use; north-west porch buttresses suggest a tower was intended

---

(a) **42,** THE OLD VICARAGE (2000) 42, THE VICARAGE (1964) 36, (1939) ROEHAMPTON

(b) 1894

(c) 1895   Miss BAILLIE
1905   H. CHRISTIE
1916   A. BENNETT
1921   Mrs H. FABER
1942   Miss SHEPHERD
1950   E. MALLINSON
1964   Canon F. CROSS
1972   Revd J. GOTT
1999* R. GUY

(g) circa 2001 refurbishment, garage added, double gabled, wood porch, stepped back north wing and single storey added. Brick with blue brick course

---

(a) *(LL)* **44,** 38, (1939), ST. STEPHENS LAWN (1900)

(b) circa 1900

(c) 1905   A. BAKER
1910   Miss BLENKIRON
1961   G. SEARIGHT

1937   Colonel T. LANGRIDGE DSO
1950   E. OULD
1957   Mrs KIRKLAND
1968   Miss V. LISTER
1999* H. CRESSWELL

(d) one of a symmetrical pair with no. 46. Bays, balcony railed, seven bedrooms, decorated carved wood pelmet above ground floor windows, pierced bargeboards, entrance porch leaded panels

(e) 1980s to 1990s a guest house

(a) *(LL)* **46,** 40, (1939), 2, ST. STEPHENS LAWN (1900)

(b) circa 1900

(c) 1905   Mrs J. COOK
1910   Colonel W. STURGES
1916   W. MOTT
1921   Revd A. HEADLEY
1927   Misses JONES
1931   Mrs DALEY
1939   Mrs BEACHER
1950   W. WEECH J.P.
1957   Revd R. CRUICKSHANK
1961   W. CAMM
1968   J. PEARSON
1978   H. HUBER

(d) Pair with no 44. Bay has no railed balcony

(g) WEECH Headmaster Sedburgh previously at 35 The Park

HUBER General manager Walker-Crosweller

(a) **48,** 48a (1968) 42, 42a (1950) 42 (1936) CAMPERDOWN

named because either:

(1) ONSLOW was a descendant of Vice Admiral who defeated the Dutch fleet off Camperdown, N. Holland and the Batavian Republic, 1797
or
(2) had served on HMS *Camperdown*, which in 1893, rammed HMS *Victoria* in exercise off Beirut, as a result of an order from Admiral Tryon to Admiral Markham being misunderstood, and 358 drowned.

(b) 1902

(c) 1903   Captain, later Rear Admiral H. ONSLOW
1907   Miss WAKEFIELD £1,700
1950   Lieutenant Colonel. R. COBOLD (42) J. WALFORD (42a)
1957   Sir G. PEARCE (42) J. WALFORD (42a)
1968   A. PHILENS (48) J. WALFORD (48a)
1999*   converted to 8 flats

(d) Red brick, stone details, blocked centre doorway, stone bay each
side with gable,decorative wood finials

(f) original stone wall on south side

(a) **50,** (1961) 44 (1957)

(b) circa 1980 on part of St. Stephens Lawn site

(c) 1957   H. STANNARD at 44
1999*   M. ROBERTSON (50A), A. MOHAN (50B), Ms R. HANBURY-BROWN (50C)
E. HOFFMAN, K. HOOPER, M. JOHNS (50D)

(f) now 4 town houses A-D. Terrace mansard roof, open porch, integral garage

(a) **52**

(b) circa 1939

(c) 1968   W. CAMM
1999*   S. BOOKER

(d) Brick Two storey Centre gable. Hipped roof. First floor windows shuttered

(f) Wall to road stucco over brick, probably older than house

(a) **54**

(b) circa 1940

(c) 1961   D. HARRIES
1999*   Miss E.E.M. HARRIES

(d) Brick. Gable at north end of façade. Integral garage. Entrance flush

(a) **56**

(b) 1957

(c) 1999*   Ms S. BISHOP

(d) in a terrace of four two storey rendered town houses

(a) **58**

(c) 1999*   T. SMITH

(d) As for no 56

(a) *(SL)* **59 PARKFIELD LAWN** (1870), PARKFIELD (1860)

(b) 1845   unfinished state

(c) 1860   Mrs WHITTINGSTALL
    1865   Captain J.W. ALLEN
    1890   W. BIRD
    1895   Misses NOYES
    1900   Colonel G. NOYES RA
    1927   Mrs PARK
    1933   Mrs PARK, G. WATHEN
    1950   Mrs COOPER
    1957   Mrs JONES
    1968   G. HEPWORTH, Miss HOMER
    1999*   A. STEWART (1) W. PALMER (2) K. GRINDLE (3) J. TENNENT (4)

(d) Pair with Park Gate, but with tower on the north end

(e) 1957   guest house
    1968   flats

(g) NOYES family "society" weddings at St Stephens, military background

   ALLEN Lieutenant Colonel 1876. Trinity College Cambridge. Drawing Master at
   Cheltenham College 1882-7. Family First World War service includes Captain J.F. won
   MC, Captain E.H.N and Brigadier General A.J.N became CB. Died 1906

(a) **60**

(c) 1999*   Ms R. STEVENSON

(d) As for no 56

(a) *(SL)* **61 PARK GATE** (1860)

(b) 1845

(c) 1855   Colonel DIGGLE
1865   C. CRISPIGNEY
1870   Major FOY
1885   Mrs FOY
1900   Miss COXWELL ROGERS
1936   C. MAY
1939   Mrs A. PERKIN
1957   P. VINCE
1961   W. BAWDEN
1999*   J. DAVIES

(d) Wide eaves, original windows centre are corniced on brackets

(e) flats 1961

(g) gate piers

(a) **62**

(c) 1957   Mrs REED
           Mrs CARLTON
1999*   G. GARVEY

(d) As for no. 56

(a) **63** attached to REDESDALE HOUSE The Park

(c) 1999*   A. JENNINGS, Ms F. SANDERS (1), W. PARKIN (2)
2007   M. WHITE (1), D. PARKIN (2)

(a) **64**

(c) 1939   Mrs D. DENNIS
1950   Mrs DENNIS Flat 1; Squadron Leader D. PREDY DFC GM (Flat 2)
1957   Mrs DENNIS, C. BROWN
1968   Mrs DENNIS, Mrs BROWN
1999*   N. MACASKILL

(d) Stucco. Double fronted detached two storey. Gabled breakforward. North has full height bow windows, south has square. Centre porch tiled canopy

(a) **66**

(b) circa 1960

(c) 1961   A. STRAIN
    1968   R. MUIRIE
    1975   C. HARRIS, E. KENDALL
    1999* D. HOLMER, Ms B. WILSON

(d) terrace three storey town houses, integral garage

(a) **68**

(b) circa 1960

(c) 1961   A. DISS
    1968   H. THOMSON
    1   S. HOOLE
    1999* M. FREEDMAN

(d) as for 66

(a) **70**

(b) circa 1960

(c) 1961   Mrs D. WRIGHT
    1975   B. MONK
    1999* P. JAY

(d) as for 66

(a) *(SL)* **ST. STEPHENS MANOR** (1879), LITTLE HATHERLEY (1857), HATHERLEY VILLA (1843)

(b) 1847   land owned by C.J. BIRD

(c) 1847   C. BIRD
    1965   Captain ROBERTS
    1870   C. BIRD
    1880   Mrs BIRD
    1881   Misses BIRD
    1887   Revd C. MCARTHUR
    1891   J. GRAFTON-ROSS
    c1905 Revd C. MACARTHUR
    1906   Colonel R. ROGERS JP
    1916   A. PINHEY ICS

    1921   Mrs F. PALMER

    1927   G. JOBLING

    1936   Colonel R. HART DSO

    1950   L. NORTHCROFT

    1980   Flats

(d) Tudor style. Bargeboard gable, "school room, smoking room" 1899

(e) 2005 Conversion to apartments £400,000

(f) Sale 1879 "attractive gardens, lake, stabling, coach house, long winding carriage drive"

    1980 building land developed for 9 chalet bungalows

(g) MCARTHUR first vicar of St. Stephens, who bought house as private accommodation

    ROGERS dentist, Honorary Colonel of Volunteers, mayor 1895-7, county councillor

    NORTHCROFT engineer with Armstrong Whitworth, chairman and managing director Spirax Sarco

(g) grounds used by HUDSON to host church events, including boating on lake, display of poultry and large flock of guinea pigs

GRAFTON ROAD

I F THE PARK has been a flexible term, embracing at one time or another, Park Place and Moorend Park Road, the word Grafton has been interchangeable too with Gratton. Add to this 'Argyle' and the confusion is complete.

To help sort out: in 1826 Grafton Street was its name, but the designation applied only east of Painswick Road; indeed until 1891 the western part had been called Argyle Place, with the eastern length being Grafton Road in 1839, and The Grafton Road on the 1864 map. Even the word Grafton derives from Grotten hence Gratton, and may refer to stubble, or stony ground, or describe a stream – in this case the Westall Brook.

Whatever uncertainties abound about meaning, they can be put to one side in appreciating the character of the road. Visually it reflects that of The Park, with its grass verges also enjoying the presence of mature trees at least in its western part.

Here too are fine examples of villas standing in large gardens: Crofton Lodge, Westbourne House and No 11, formerly Mosborough/ Brandon Villa. Admittedly Brandon House, Heysham House, Greville Lodge and Villa properly belong to intersecting roads, but they justify inclusion in Grafton Road for their significant contribution to the 'streetscape'. The north side has a different character: a short terrace of four somewhat disjointed properties - nine were intended – engaging in their haphazard facades and roof line yet including at least a delightful fan light, and a rear bow. Nor should the pairs of 19th century and more recent villas be undervalued.

The eastern end is not without its interest, crossing as it does the route of the railroad from Leckhampton quarries. Admittedly the Grafton Brewery has gone, but on the opposite corner with Norwood Road there is still the fascia panel of Watts & Son whose coach building business flourished a century ago.

Finally, providing a focus from either direction is the church of St. Philip & St. James occupying a central site once called Graftons, that has had a church since 1838.

(a) *(LL)* **2, 1** ARGYLE PLACE

(b) 1840

(c) 1840   Mrs MONRO
    1851**   Mrs M. SCHOLEFIELD and 3 daughters, 1 son, cook, housemaid
    1871   Mrs J. HAY
    1876   Mrs MCK. RYND
    1887   C.B. ATHURTON
    1902   Captain F. TRAVERS
    1911   Mrs B. GARDNER
    1921   E.C. NOTON
    1927   B.C. KENNEDY
    1942   Mrs H.W. GARRARD, H.L. ANLEY
          (2A) Mrs S. PATERSON
    1950   P.J. MORAN, C.H. ROBERTS, Mrs KNOWLES
          (2A) Lieutenant Colonel A.A. BONTOR
    1957   A.G.E. AMES, A.S.P. WILLIAMS
          (2A) Lieutenant Colonel A.A. BONTOR, Mrs KNOWLES
    1961   Mrs E.L. COCKING, G.F.M. RUFFORD, A.J. ZEAL
    1968   Mrs E.L. COCKING, A.J. ZEAL, K.K. RUFFORD
    1975   Mrs E.L. COCKING, H.F. WALKER
    1999*   D. ILES, (top floor flat) K. IRELAND

(a) *(SL)* **3, CROFTON LODGE** (1911)
GRAFTON LAWN

(b) circa 1820-50

(c)
1876	Colonel BROWN
1887	Admiral ALEXANDER
1902	J.F. MUIR JP
1925	Lady A.M. WAPSHARE wife of Lieutenant General Sir RICHARD WAPSHARE KCIE, CB, CSI
1936	Major General L.W. JACKSON CB, CSI, DSO
1942	Mrs H.W. JACKSON
1961	Mrs E.M. JACKSON
1971	D.H. GORDON-POWELL
1973	I.M. BAMLETT
1975	E.C. BUCK, N.R. SINCLAIR
1984	T. HILL and 5 flats

(d) Villa stucco over brick. Two/three storey and basement. Distyle Ionic porch. Conservatory 1910 at east. Ground floor balcony double scroll motif.

(f) Piers and wall

(g) HILL was at the BBC from 1942 until retiring in 1983 as Assistant Head of Network Radio. He worked as producer, writer and director.

(a) *(LL)* **4,** 2 ARGYLE PLACE

(b) circa 1840

(c)
1838	Major ROBERTS
1851**	J. COWMAN age 77 'pauper'
1871	Misses GREY
1902	Miss GREY
1911	Misses GREY
1921	Miss GREY
1930	Mrs STEWART
1939	F.C. GREY
1950	Mrs J.M. MACPHERSON
1957	Mrs POWELL, Miss J.M. MACPHERSON
1961	K.F. APPS
1968	J.R. MACCALL

1972   J.D. GILLIES
1999*   B. MAUGHFLING

(d) fanlight has original glass

(a) *(LL)* **6,** 3 ARGYLE PLACE

(b) circa 1840

(c) 1840   R. COMFIELD
1851** Mrs M. FISON, daughter, 'maid of all work', gardener
1871   G. CRANE
1887   Miss PANTING
1902   R. H. MARTIN
1921   Miss E. HERBERT
1927   Revd C. S. PARKER
1930   Mrs C. S. PARKER
1957   K.G. WHITE
1961   R.B HENTY
1975   A. J. SMITH
1996*   E. WEBB, Ms B. DAY

(a) *(LL)* **8,** 4 ARGYLE PLACE

(b) 1840

(c) 1851** No entry
1871   Captain T. L. CHAMPION
1876   Captain BUCKLE
1878   CUZNER
1887   Revd J. W. HART
1902   Miss LYNNE
1921   Miss TWEEDIE
1927   Major A. P. POE
1942   A. JONES
1961   Mrs A. JONES
1968   M. JONES
1999*   M. JONES

(a) *(LL)* **9, WESTBOURNE HOUSE**, BRYNEAM (1902), WESTBOURNE LODGE (1876)

(b) Mid nineteenth century

(c) 1876   Revd H. HUTCHINSON
1902   P. REYNOLDS

1921   Ms F. E. DAVIDSON
1927   Mrs POWELL
1936   Misses POWELL
1957   I. B. COOKE
1961   G.H. TURNER
1998   G. HONEYBILL

(d) Detached villa. Two storeys and basement. Stucco on brick. Central round - arched entrance. Recessed doorway. Stone balustered steps. Shallow breakforward bays each side full height. Ground floor pilastered windows. Iron work balcony. Second floor double round – headed windows. Cornice. Wide eaves.

(a) *(LL)* **10,** 1 ARGYLE VILLAS

(b) Mid nineteenth century

(c) 1871   Major General J. D. KENNEDY
     1887   W. C. P. GRANT R N
     1902   Miss E. HENRY
     1939   Mrs J. OWEN, Miss TROLLOPE
     1942   Lieutenant Colonel E. H. REES-WEBBE
     1950   D.R.P. RAYMOND (10a) Mrs C. E. Butler
     1957   Major F. L. HACKING
     1971   P.S. HAVERY
     1999*   G. HOOD, Ms J. GLOAG

(d) Pair with no 12, semi-detached villas. Two storey and basement. Set back corner entrance porch. Then canted ground floor with circle parapet on decorated brackets. Window surrounds entablatured, first floor segmental depressed, sills on foliated brackets. Bracketed eaves.

(a) *(SL)* **11, MOSBOROUGH (1921)** INCHYRA situated 4 miles east of Perth, on north bank of River Tay, BRANDON VILLA (1829)

(b) circa 1840

(c) 1850   Mrs W. M. RAIKES
     1871   T.OXLEY
     1878   Major General COX
     1910   F. CADE
     1921   Lieutenant Colonel E. BENNETT
     1927   A. B. STEWART
     1939   Colonel P. P. KILKELLY
     1950   Brigadier General T. BRUCE
              CMG DSO
     1968   E. P. C. BRUCE

1971   D. H. J. MARTIN-JONES-PEACHEY

1993   M. GRAN, C. JAMES

(d) Circa 1985 divided 11 & 11 B by excavating under west conservatory to provide garage, and combining west half of main house. Originally two storey plus attic. Stucco over brick. Quoins at ground floor ends. Wide eaves to flattened roof. Windows eared architraves – central porch pilastered with sunk panel. East breakforward with ground floor bow.

(g) CADE Headmaster Junior Department Cheltenham College

GRAN writer for television

(a) *(LL)* **12,** 2 ARGYLE VILLAS

(b) Mid nineteenth century

(c) 1871   Sir W. BURTON

1873   Mrs TATUM

1876   Mrs General SHULDHAM

1902   Mrs G. F. SHULDHAM

1927   Miss GREEN, Revd E. W. SOUTH

1930   W. McC. NICHOLSON

1939   Sir G. A. EVANS-FREKE Bart

1942   Mrs G. B. DEIGHTON

1968   V. VINCENT

1999*   T. DIXON; A. FRENCH, A. PALFRY, Ms D. SWELL

(d) As no 10

(a) *(SL)* **60, CHURCH HOUSE (1967),** S. PHILIPS LODGE

(b) circa 1840-60

(c) 18--   Mrs WHITE

1865   Commander T. TICKNELL R N

1876   Lieutenant Colonel. E. J. TICKNELL

1928   Mrs N. T. PRICE

1942   T.T. PRICE (Herefordshire farmer)

1946   Miss A. M. D. PRICE to W. J. MOOR BUILDER

1967   GLOUCESTER DIOCESAN TRUST LTD. and Parochial Church Council of SS PHILIP and JAMES CHURCH

(d) Stucco over brick. Two storey Plus attic and basement. Quions, moulded ground-floor sill band. Windows tooled architraves. South porch round arch, cornice, low parapet extension south 1960's.

(e) Converted to communal rooms for parochial use, flats, children's playgroup

(f) Car park for church users, children's play area

(a) *(L)* **62 PAINSWICK ROAD, BRANDON HOUSE,**
BADGEWORTH COURT SCHOOL (1930s),
BRANDON VILLA (1902) Brandon a family name of Tryes

(b) circa 1825 for H. B. Trye; architect, J. Forbes

(c)
1838	H. TRYE
1840	W. READE
1843	Countess DE PONTHIEU
1849	Archbishop WHATLEY
----	Admiral MCKELLAR
1851**	C.C. HAY, wife, six children, four servants, butler
1854	Captain STEVENSON
1855	Captain READ
1859	Mrs F. MYERS
1902	Major General COX
1912	E. R. GURNEY
1930s	Badgeworth Court Special School Group Home for Boys
1936	Sale of school £3,000 four reception and two classrooms, changing room, gym. "910ft building land"
1940	Let to Government
1957	Tungum Co engineers formerly of White House Arle Rd
1987	J. HAWTIN builder. Brandon House Ltd for £305,000. J.J.H. Homes. let to TARGET Public Relations firm

(d) Ashlar, 2 storey. End bays breakforward. Centre porch wreathed, tetrastyle composite capitals. Corinthian capitals on pilasters similar to those at 121, 123, 125 and 127 Promenade. Probably Coade stone details.

(e) 1930s special school for boys. 1940 Government offices. 1957 engineering. 1987 builders.

(f) Piers. 1936 garden extended 400ft to Tryes Road: lawns, playground 'well-hidden from road', outhouse "magnificent rockery of Cotswold stone, including 7 Brandon Place suitable for gardener or chauffeur"

(g) HAY of Scottish descent, was a governor of Cheltenham College.

WHATELEY archbishop of Dublin 1831, professor of political economy, Oxford 1829, opposer of Tractarians, supported Catholic emancipation; caustic, outspoken, died 1863.

(a) *(SL)* **ST. PHILIP & ST. JAMES** (1882) ST. PHILIP (1838)

(b) Philip 1838-40 E. Shellard architect £2,500
St. Philip & James 1879-82 J. Middleton architect £9,700

(c) Incumbents

 1843 J.E. RIDDLE (St Philip, 1840)
 1859 J.L. HARRISON (St Philip)
 1869 W. H. HUTCHINSON
 1912 R. A. HAY
 1931 J. M. BALLARD
 1940 O. D. PARKER
 1959 E. H. EYNON
 1981 D. NYE
 1996 P. CHICKEN
 2007 I. BUSSELL

(d) Original church being "inadequate for the improved wealthy neighbourhood" was enlarged first by new chancel and subsequently nave and tower. Intended spire substituted by saddleback and flèche 1903. Exterior hard rusticated stone. Style Early English. Interior rich chancel. Iron screen.

(a) *(SL)* **36, GRATTON ROAD**: GREVILLE LODGE GREVILLE VILLA
Greville family, lord of manor of Ashley, Charlton Kings

(b) 1825-26 contemporary with Greville House, making complementary pair.

(c) 1826 T. WILLIAMS
 1835 Mrs. General PALMER
 1838 Mrs. WRAY
 1845 C. CRIPPS
 1848 Mrs. H. FORSTER
 1851** Mrs. S. H. FORSTER, 1 servant
 1857 Mrs. WRAY
 1861** Mrs Martha WRAY, daughter, 2 servants
 1867 H. DAVIES purchaser
 1870 Revd. J.H. CARDEW
 1871** CARDEW, 5 children, 2 servants
 1881** 'to let' R. TROVEY coach painter, wife dressmaker
 1883 T. WILKINS grocer

1891** WILKINS, 6 children, 2 servants
1897 Mrs. LUCAS
1901** E. COCKS-JOHNSTON surgeon, daughter, nurse, cook, housemaid
1905 Dr J.D. PEARSON
1927 Dr W.H. PEDLOW
1954 Mrs E.W. Browning
1965 J.A. HANCOX
1975 Mrs S. HANCOX
2006 P. VOLCER

(d) original house, 3 bay, central porch; east extension 1827. South extension, porch moved to it, and additional floor for servants 1868. Bay added to façade 1890. Further south extension with bay 1928. Extensively renovated 2006. Porch Ionic with railings having concave scrolled lozenge motif.

(f) Coach house giving on to Edward Street 1890s.

(g) DAVIES Town commissioner, editor *Cheltenham Chronicle* proprietor, *Looker On* lived at Harley Lodge , Tivoli Road

CARDEW chaplain General Hospital, & Union Workhouse Cooks

COCKS-JOHNSTON medical officer Delancey Hospital

HANCOX bookseller and on many occasions between 1970 and 1990 Director of Cheltenham Festival of Literature.

(a) *(SL)* **37, GRATTON ROAD**: GREVILLE HOUSE

(b) circa 1820-30 built for H.N.TRYE

(c) 1835 H.N. TRYE
1841 J. PIERSON
1846 Major E HAMILTON East India Company
1851** Major E.F. HAMILTON E.I.C.S wife, housemaid, two cooks
1857 Lieutenant Colonel HAMILTON
1863 Mrs. A. VICKERS, Miss. E. PARRY
1871 Miss PARRY
1889 Lieutenant Colonel W.B. LOGAN, Major J.R. HOLLAND
1896 Misses HAMILTON
1936 A.G BISHOP
WWll T.R. THOMAS
1947 Air Registration Board £4,500
2002 development of Morgans Drive, restoring house to domestic use

(d) Stucco over brick. 2 storey. North-east corner curved. Blind windows on ground and first floor. Centre porch on east distylic Ionic, elaborate fan light. A complementary villa to Greville Lodge on opposite side of Painswick Road.

(e) Printing department for Civil Aviation Authority, 1947

(f) Railings, pier incised panels, frieze incised lozenge, pyramid caps

(g) BISHOP housemaster Cheltenham College

THOMAS first secretary of Air Registration Board

(a) **23, S. PHILIPS COTTAGE** (1939)

(c) 1911   W. MUCKLEY
    1921   MS K.E. MUCKLEY
    1927   VINCENT and PILKINGTON motor engineers
    1930   P.W. VINCENT motor engineer
    1971   N. VINCENT

(d) Demolished with re-development of Edward street

(a) **24,** GRAFTON HOUSE (1933)

(c) 1957   D.L. TURNER & sons, builders
    1961   T.C. SAFE builders yard

(a) **26,** GRAFTON BREWERY OFFICE (1921) OLD GRAFTON HOUSE (1927) NAILSWORTH BREWERY STORES (1911)

(b) 1840-50

(c) 1851** F.MARTINDALE brewer employing one man, wife, three   daughters, one servant
    1911   J.B. TILL
    1921   J.B. TILL
    1942   Mrs. J. MILL
    1950   A.J. TAYLOR
    1961   A.J. TAYLOR, J.F. LACHLAN
    1999*   D. MASON

(d) Two storeys plus basement, canted bay ground floor and basement. Stucco.

(a) **28,** GRAFTON HOUSE

(b) 1840-50

(c) 1862   converted to brewery by Ashby Saunders, contravening covenant of Billings
    1911   Mrs. A. FRANKLIN
    1921   Miss. G.F. BEST
    1927   Miss. G.F. BEST, J.B. TILL (Old Grafton House)
    1933   J.B. TILL, Miss. G.F. BEST
    1939   J.B. TILL
    1950   Mrs. M. TILL
    1963   C.W. LAWRENCE, L.A. GODDARD
    1971   E. PARRY, J. CHAPLIN
    1973   W.E. RADFORD, N.M. TREBILCOCK
    1975   W.E. RADFORD
    1999*   Ms M. LACEY, Ms A. GOODRUN, Ms K. FEWELL

(d) Two storey and basement adjoining no 26, chamfered corner with Norwood Rd. Stucco in brick. Hipped roof behind parapet.

(a) **GRAFTON COURT**, NORWOOD STREET,
GRAFTON CARRIAGE WORKS (1921)

(c) 1911   G.H. WATTS carriage and coach builders
            Norwood St

Western Estates converted to 10 apartments

(a) **30, HILL VIEW** (1936)

(c) 1911   W. BUBB
    1930   A.W. WYLIE
    1933   H.G. GRIFFITHS
    1942   Mrs. D.O. GRIFFITHS
    1999*   Ms. B. GRANT

(d) Two storey, canted ground floor bay.

(a) **32**

(b) 1840-50

(c) 1927   W.F.B.SELLEY furniture remover
    1936   SELLEY & sons furniture removers, A.HARVEY blacksmith
    1950   SELLEY & sons furniture removers

(d) Rebuilt to provide large entrance for vans. Small doorway to west & first floor windows. Adjacent to no. 30

(a) **34, S.PHILIPS MEWS**

(c) 1916   W.SMITH
    1936   SELLEY & son furniture removers. A.HARVEY blacksmith
    1957   D.S.SELLEY
    1999*   D.F.SELLEY

(d) Two storeys. Arched entrance. Adjacent to no. 32

Argyle Place

ASHFORD ROAD

S TRETCHING FROM TIVOLI Road to Gratton Road, the thoroughfare did not receive its present name officially till 1891. The section between Park Place and Painswick Road was in 1834 known as Lower Grafton Street; being described as an entirely new street by the *Looker-On* a year later.

The substantial terrace on the south side of the street perpetuates the name Grafton. Of its six houses only two are reported as being built by 1838, the remainder following in the next four years.

Smaller than their neighbours but of equal respectability as the *Looker-On* described it in 1835, on the north side the houses of Andover Terrace take their name from the courtesy title of the Earl of Suffolk's eldest son. Here again the building was slow, only three of the five being included in the 1844 directory. Andover House, the oldest pair together with its easterly neighbours completes a coherent range of ten houses, while the western section of the road presents a more fragmentary streetscape with the large pair of Ashford House and Court set back, competing with the exuberant mix of classical, Gothic and Tyrolean styles vying for attention on the opposite side of the road.

Today Ashford Road merges into Gratton Road, instead of linking directly with Bath Road via S.Philip's Street, but perhaps its history shows greater association with the original fields called Grotten.

Although not strictly a 'Feeder' to The Park its close affinity geographically and architecturally to Park Place, and Tivoli Road merits its inclusion here.

(a) *(SL)* **1 FOX HOUSE** "we saw a fox in the garden" (2004) FLEURVILLE

(b) 1850

(c) 1864   W. BROWN housemaster

     1878   R.P. SMITH housemaster

     1916   A. ROGERSON also owned 18 Tivoli Road which he sold with its coach house and 'use of part of garden of Fleurville' to Edwin Osbaldeston-Mitford in 1908 for £1750

     1955   A.S. LANE to E.A. WILKINSON £3,650

     1957   E.A. SWINDEN executor of Wilkinson

     1961   House divided into 3 dwellings: MRS D. GREEN (1) MRS H. MILLINGTON-BUCK, Mrs K. HILL (1A)

     1987   Bushurst Properties £103,000

     1990   J. FERRIS – Mrs FIRMIN (1A)

     1999*   J. LITTLE

     2004   R. SETTATREE gynaecological surgeon (Fox House)

(d) Originally one villa. Stucco on brick. Fish scale slate roof. Two storeys. One storey entrance porch on east with pierced balcony. Fluted pilasters. Windows hood mouldings. Tyrolean barge-boards with finials. West octagonal turret with decorative panels and weather vane. Secondary hooded entrance at west return

"An idiosyncratic mix of Italianate, Swiss & Tudor Revival" – *SL*. Bargeboard design identical with those at 124/6 The Park.

(f) 2007   Gate piers

(e) 1864-79 Cheltenham College Private Boarding House

     1963   Majestic Hotel staff annexe

(g) WILKINSON manager of Majestic Hotel, Park Place

(a) **LYNCROFT (1979)** 2 PICTON HOUSE (1977), KENBILL GARDENS (1971)

(b) 1950s

(c) 1953   C.V. SHADWELL 'kitchen garden adjoining Fleurville'
    1971   R.M. MANNING
    1977   A. RODGER

(d) As for number 3 but rendered

(f) South west corner wood structure quadripartite roof, decorative bargeboards, probably nineteenth century.

(a) *(LL)* **2, ASHFORD HOUSE**, ASHFORD (1916)

(b) 1840

(c) 1911   Mrs TREVALDWYN
    1927   Viscountess SELBY, Miss SHAW-PHILLIPS
    1936   Miss LANGDALE
    1942   Mrs G.W. HEDLEY
    1968   Miss EDGSON
    1971   H. ADLAM, M. DUNN, A.THOMAS
    1975   H. ADLAM, M. DUNN
    1999* 8 Flats

(a) **3, THE CREEK**

(c) 1957   A.DAVIES
    1961   H.S. MCKENZIE
    1973   S.J. MARTIN
    1999* R. PENTYCROSS

(d) Semi-detached pair with Lyncroft

(f) magnolia

(a) *(LL)* **4, ASHFORD COURT**, TIXALL (1916), SANUBI

(b) 1840

(c) 1911   Mrs C. ASTON
    1942   Miss N.P. JONES
    1950   T.A. SPRAGUE DSc
    1959   E.R. BAYLIS £2,800

1968   Mrs C. HALLINAN, E.R. BAYLIS

1971   E.R. BAYLIS

1999*   8 Flats

(f) In 1950s garden still extended north where now a bungalow. Lane round area. Gated wall to where now three houses

(g) JONES was Principal of St. Mary's College, though she did not live in the property on retirement, letting it to Dr SPRAGUE who had worked at the Herbarium, Kew Gardens.

(a) *(SL)* **GRAFTON TERRACE**, 1, GRAFTON TERRACE

(b) 1830

(d) Terrace of six houses had an attic storey added, distinguishing it from numbers 20 and 22 opposite. Central four bay breakforward. Windows of the ground floor have panelled aprons and cornices on consoles. Crowning cornice. Paired entrances with solid porches and incised pillars.

(a) *(SL)* **1, ELMFIELD**, 1, GRAFTON TERRACE

(b) See group entry

(c) 1850   Mrs BOWLY

1851** F. WHITTHALL retired merchant (age 29!), wife, 4yr son, nurse, cook.

1873   Mrs PARKER

1999*   Ms M.WILLIAMS

(d) See group entry

(a) *(SL)* **1, HAZELWOOD**, 2 GRAFTON TERRACE

(b) See group entry

(c) 1850   Miss ELLINTHORPE

1851** Miss C. PRICE, Mrs S. RISHTON sister, one servant

1871   Mrs EDMONDS

1873   Dr. HILLIER

1876   Mrs TAYLOR

1911   Mrs S.W. SMITH

1927   Mrs E.E. EDLMANN

1999*   S. DICKS

(d) See group entry

(a) *(SL)* **3, FERNLEIGH,** 3, GRAFTON TERRACE

(b) See group entry

(c) 1851** Mrs M. HOME, three daughters and one servant

     1871   B. REYNOLDS

     1876   Dr. HILLIER

     1887   H. BASKERVILLE

     1911   Mrs HANLON

     1921   Mrs M.W. JAMES

     1933   W. DAVEY

     1999*   Ms M. ROOKS

(d) See group entry

(a) *(SL)* **6**

(b) 1832

(c) 1921   J. HADDEN (see also 25 Park Place)

     1936   Miss SAUNDERS

     1968   Mrs M. SCOTT

     1999*   4 Flats

(d) See 27 Park Place

(e) Wood and iron verendah facing Park Place. Pier with moulded cap, 'forms good feature with corner pier to 29 Park Place' *(SL)*

(a) *(SL)* **3, OAKFIELD,** 4 GRAFTON TERRACE

(b) See group entry

(c) 1851** Mrs E. TOMKIS lodging house keeper, one son stationer, apprentice, one servant

     1871   Mrs MORRIS

     1887   G. WILLIAMS

     1911   L.T. PRICE

     1916   Mrs G.B. HODGSON

1927   Mrs JAMES
1942   P. FARR
1950   E.J. TAYLOR
1961   O. THOMAS
1999*   T. RICHARDSON

(d)   See group entry. Windows, ground and first floor have scrolled motif.

(a)   *(SL)* **8**, 23

(b)   1820-32

(c)   1933   H.L. MALONE
      1961   Miss I.G. MALONE
      1968   Mrs K.J. O'DELL, Miss I.G. MALONE
      1999*   Ms H. FINLAY, G. TOWNSEND

(d)   See 40 Park Place, central entrance recessed in round arch surround.

(a)   *(SL)* **5, ASHLEY**, 5 GRAFTON TERRACE

(b)   See group entry

(c)   1850   Mr. SPEAKMAN
      1851**   Mrs E. BIGNALL, one daughter, two nieces, Ms S. Guy, one house servant
      1871   R.H. CURZON
      1878   MISS. NEWMAN
      1887   Liuetenant O. WHEELER
      1911   Miss FRY
      1916   C. GARDINER MA
      1942   T.J.A. MAPP, chiropractor
      1950   Mrs E.M. VOSS
      1999*   P. SHARP

(d)   See group entry

(a)   *(SL)* **ANDOVER TERRACE**

(b)   circa 1830

(d)   Terrace of five houses. Stucco over ashlar. Iron balcony. Solid porches have pillars with a Greek key motif and entablature.

(a) *(SL)* **10**, 1 ANDOVER TERRACE

(b) circa 1830

(c) 1850   Mrs CLEATHER
    1855   Revd J. HEBB
    1871   J.E. COULSON
    1873   Revd J. SPILSBURY
    1887   Mr VALE
    1902   Revd W. SHOVELTON
    1921   Mrs J.SULLIVAN
    1927   Miss PHILLIPS
    1930   H.F. FOSTER
    1942   Mrs V.E. FOSTER
    1999* Ms A. DOWTY

(d) See group entry

(a) *(SL)* **5, LINDEN**, THE TERRACE (1999) 11, GRAFTON TERRACE

(b) 1830

(c) 1851** Mrs E. MORACE 4 daughters, son surgeon dentist, son, chemist pupil, 1 servant
    1871   J.J. ANNING
    1887   H. GREEN
    1911   Mr FISHER
    1916   Mrs H. FEA
    1921   Mrs S.A. WATKINS
    1927   W.J. MOORE, builder
    1950   C.T. KEBLE, private tutor
    1957   Mrs STEWART
    1963   A.C. BIFFEN
    1968   H.F. YOUNG
    1971   J.T. MEAGER
    1999* Ms K. HARDWICK, P. SEAMAN

(d) See group entry. No crowning cornice. Window boxes with embellished rods and central scrolled panel on the first floor. Iron balcony.

(a) *(SL)* **12**, 2, ANDOVER TERRACE

(b) circa 1830

(c) 1850   W.E. EVANS
     1855   Mrs SPIER
     1871   Mrs W.A. SERLE
     1887   H. BRANDT
     1916   Miss PENNO
     1930   Mrs L. PENNO
     1933   K. WARE
     1939   Mrs F.L.WOODIN
     1950   A. MERCATI
     1957   A. SHAW
     1971   M.A. MYRING
     1975   M.A. LEA, RJ. HERBERT
     1999* R. O'CONNOR, R. EDWARDS, S. FINCHER

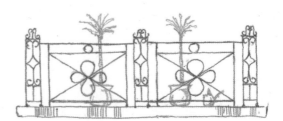

(d) See group entry. Iron balcony with quatrefoil motif.

(a) **13, BRANDON COTTAGES**

(c) 1927   Mrs S. PHILLIPS
     1930   Mrs E. SHILL
     1936   Mrs WEST
     1957   Miss WEST

(a) *(SL)* **14**, 3, ANDOVER TERRACE

(b) circa 1830

(c) 1850   A. BOUZY
     1971   G. HOOK
     1873   Mlle MOISSONIER
     1887   Mr CORNELIUS
     1927   V.G. SAUNDERS
     1933   Mrs BARRETT
     1975   D.S. HUGHES
     1999* D. HUGHES

(d) See group entry

(a) **15, BRANDON COTTAGES**

(c) 1927   A.E. ATTWOOD
1957   W.S. ALLEN
1961   H. HAINES

(a) *(SL)* **16**, 4 ANDOVER TERRACE

(b) circa 1830

(c) 1850   T. WRIGHT
1855   W. DOWDING
1871   Miss A. GARRETT
1887   Mr. TEAGUE, M.H. WHISH
1902   Mrs MCLAREN
1921   Mrs F. LEACH
1939   A.R. WILSON
1950   Mrs WILSON
1961   Mrs S.J. FITZGERALD
1968   D.J. HATFIELD, T. CRUTTENDON, E.J. PAYNE
1971   J.L. MITCHELL, R.N. ILLINGWORTH, G.A. HARDWICK, J.DOWNER
1973   C.A. GRIFFITH
1999*   Ms A. SHAW, Ms M. CLARKE, A. FREER

(d) See group entry

(a) *(SL)* **18**, 5 ANDOVER TERRACE, THE COT (1921), PARK LODGE (1871)

(b) circa 1830

(c) 1850   Mrs FRASER
1871   C.R. HILL
1873   Mrs HILL
1902   Miss HILL
1921   Mrs LEISHMAN
1930   I. MORGAN
1936   H.F. MARTYN
1942   Mrs MARTYN
1950   Miss JOHNSON
1975   M.C. STORR

1999* P. TARLING, (18B) Ms T. BREWSTER

(d) See group entry

(a) *(SL)* **20, EGERTON** (1902), 6 ANDOVER TERRACE

(b) 1820-50

(c) 1850   J.G. WILLIAMS, artist
     1871   J. BENNETT
     1880s   J.A. PROBERT
     1916   Miss TEAKLE
     1921   Dr L. PAULLEY MRCS, JP
     1950   Miss YALDWYN
     1957   Miss SHIPWAY
     1961   Mrs B. SHIPWAY
     1968   Mrs B. SHIPWAY, N.E. CLISBY, M.E. GRAHAM
     1971   H.J. HUTTON
     1975   R.V. MARKLEW
     1999*   Ms K. BYERS, homeopath

(d) Pair of houses with number 22. Ashlar façade.
     Three storeys. Doric pilasters to corners. Frieze
     and cornice and further cornice above third storey.
     Central shared door case with puny pairs of
     Tuscan pilasters.

(a) *(SL)* **22, ANDOVER HOUSE** (1871),
     7 ANDOVER TERRACE

(b) 1820-50

(c) 1871   Dr HILLIER
     1880   O. ANDREWS to E.C. GALLOP
     1886   E.C. GALLOP to W. HOWLETT £300
     1902   Misses FAITHFULL
     1909   Mrs M.L. HOWLETT
     1916   C.T. MITCHELL
     1927   Mrs HOWLETT
     1941   Mrs L.S. HONEYSETT to Mrs M.T. HALLIWELL
     1942   W.N. HALLIWELL
     1964   M. SHINN, artist
     1966   GLOUCESTERSHIRE DIOCESAN TRUST

1971   F.G. DEACON

1973   C. JARMAN

1975   D.H. PARISH to L.R. SHORT

1990   P. HARRIS, landscape architect

1999* J. CAPPER

----   P. SANDERSON, professional rugby player for Worcestershire and England

(d) As for no 20

(a) **24**, 8 CASTLEMAINE VILLA

(b) circa 1880

(c) 1916   Mrs WAKEFIELD

1921   C.A. PUGH

1933   J. MACGEORGE

1936   P.E. CYPHER

1939   W.G. THOMAS

1942   Mrs M.A. HOOK

1957   A.S. HOOK

1999* (Garden flat) MS A. SHEPHERD, R. WILLIAMS, (2) S. JANZEN, (3) M.RAYNER

(d) Pair of semi-detached villas with no 26. Stucco. Centre entrance two storey on basement.

(a) **26**, 9 COLLINGWOOD VILLA (1902)

(b) circa 1880

(c) 1902   Mrs C. PHILLIPPS

1916   H. DREDGE

1921   Miss WAKEFIELD

1927   Misses WAKEFIELD

1930   R.W.P. SMITH

1933   Mrs DENTON

1936   G.M. MAY

1939   J.M. TANDY

1942   J.M. TANDY, C.R. HOBBS

1950   C.R. HOBBS

1961   H.J. LEESON

1999* H. LEESON (Garden flat) K. HUGHES

(d) As for no 24

(a) **28**, 10

(b) circa 1850

(c) 1902   C. ROBERTS
     1916   H. LANGDOWN
     1921   C.J. GIBB
     1927   G.F. RYLAND
     1936   Mrs ROGERS
     1939   Miss A.E. HOOPER, Miss E. MURRELL
     1942   Miss E. MURRELL
     1950   Mrs E.G. ROOKE
     1999* Ms M. STLEGER-ATTENBOROUGH

(d) Conjoined to no 26 and on the east. Two storeys. Stucco

(a) **30**, CROOME VILLA

(b) 1840-50

(c) 1902   F. PARRY
     1921   Ms L.L. PARRY
     1927   F.P. PARRY
     1942   A.L. WALTON
     1957   P.F. PARRY
     1999* A. FIELDS

MOOREND PARK ROAD

ALTHOUGH THE GREATER part of the road has a mix of Edwardian and later building, the short stretch between Shurdington Road and The Park retains something of the character of the latter to justify its inclusion.

Despite the gross insertion of Dorchester Court flats where St Clair once stood, the presence of Pine Lodge and South Lawn together with former Moorend Park Hotel (former Park Grange), maintain the villa tradition of The Park, and most importantly, with the magnificent conifer at the corner of Shurdington Road, the sylvan component.

Historically too, Moorend Park Road preserves the axis of the original avenue that is shown on Merrett's 1834 map running across The Park from the still-existing gateway.

(a) **DORCHESTER COURT**

(b) 1964, developer LAPPER

(c) Twelve flats

(d) Brick. Five floors. Balconies at corners. The entrance is on the west side. Built on the site of St. Clair, The Park

(a) **LITTLE GARTH**, LITTLE COT

(b) 1840

(c) 1955   W.A. BIRCH
    1959   (Mrs. M.J. COWPER), B.C. COWPER solicitor
    1968   A. CHERRINGTON
    1971   F.J. GRIFFIN
    1999* H. MANSFIELD

(d) Single storey former coach house to Park Lawn. Extended in 2006

(a) **4, PINE LODGE** (1920), PINE VILLA (1864)

(b) Mid nineteenth century

(c) 1864   T. ASPLAND to W. GRIMSHAW £1,600
    1920   W. GRIMSHAW deceased to Mrs. E. GOGARTY
    1921   Colonel R.F. PEARSON)
    1925   Mrs. E.L. SAUNDERS
    -     Mrs E.M. STENHOUSE
    1934   Colonel F.R. DRAKE
    1938   Misses H. and E.H. GOOLDEN
    1946   Miss E. ROOK-GREEN
    1947   Miss D.B. FABER
    1975   A. SAVVIDES
    1976   C.V.D. FORRINGTON
    1982   conversion to seven flats.

(d) Detached two storey house with bow and basement. Stucco. The ground floor windows on bow have blind boxes. The North window has a canopy supported by iron work struts. The entrance is narrow arch chamfered with a simple fanlight. The pilasters are recessed panel with a deep string course. Wide eaves except on north.

(g) DRAKE claimed descent from Sir Francis

FABER related to the publishers: Mrs. Faber occupier 1950; Misses Faber afterwards.

(a) *(SL)* **6, SOUTH LAWN**

(b) circa 1820-50

(c) 1921   Ms. J.M. BOND
    1936   T.A.WHITTINGTON BA,
          private tutor; S.G. SHIMMIN
    1957   Mrs B. JACKSON
    1961   K.L. OWEN
    1971   W. FLETCHER
    1999*   J. GREEN

(d) Pair of semi-detached houses, the other half
being no 67 Shurdington Rd, Painswick Lodge.
Stucco over brick. Two storey. Doric end pilasters.
Central porch paired pilasters

(f) Railings. Extensive renovation of the garden including boundary wall and piers.

A fine evergreen tree at the junction with Shurdington Road.

(a) *(LL)* **ARKLE HOUSE** (2010), 11, MOOREND PARK HOTEL (1988),
PARK GRANGE (1921)

(b) Early twentieth century

(c) 1921   Mrs. H.R. MANSFIELD
    1957   A. HODSON, F. SMITH, Mrs. M. SULLINGS
    1961   A.W. HODGSON, Mrs. KERSHAW, B.W. TAYLOR
    1963   S. KERSHAW, J. JARVIS
    1968   St. Mary's Training College hostel
    1971   M.P. SCOTT
          North Gloucestershire Technical College
          Hostel for the Homeless
    1988   M. PENEDO
    1993   D. AKEHURST
    1998   - HARRIS
    1999   W. BUNT
    2006   T. ELLIOT

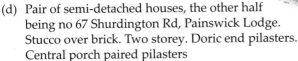

(d) Detached two storey house with basement and attic. Stucco. The façade to Moorend
Park road has arched entrance under oriel window. A canted bay on the ground floor
with arched windows. Quoined corner to Shurdington road façade which has similar
canted bay, Breakforward to gable has triple ground floor window under architrave.
Further triple windows above and in gable.

(e) 1968 College Annexe. Hostel. 1988 hotel till 2009 conversion to eleven flats

(a) **WATERFORD COURT** on the site of LECKHAMPTON HALL (1927)
LECKHAMPTON LODGE (1921)

(b) 1982

(c) 1921   Mrs E. CRESSWELL
1927   Mrs. MURRAY-RUST; Mrs. CORBISHLEY
1930   J. SAINT-HOWARD; Mrs. W. WARNER
1933   L.H. LONGLEY
1982   demolished; Waterford Court built

(e) U-shape with breakforwards on road facades. Forty five apartments. Three floors and a mansard attic. The ground floor is brick. Upper rendered

---

(a) *(LL)* **THE ROWANS**, SHURDINGTON ROAD

(b) 1868

(c) 1933   Major S. MENZIES
1950   R.S. WALKER proprietor. residential nursery:

(d) Brick. Three storey. 'Middleton' style

(e) A hostel for children of ex-patriots. Second World War, US Airforce Officers club. 1950s North Gloucestershire Technical College annexe for hotel catering and nursery nurses. In 1991 it was the BBC venue for the comedy thriller 'Dead Romantic' being renamed Garrett College of Language & Literature: temporary conservatory built.

A 1930s view looking towards The Park showing Leckhampton Hall in the foreground where Waterford Court now stands, and St Clair where Dorchester Court is today. In the background Broadlands can be seen.

To know one place well is better than to know many a little

Appendices

An Outline Chronology

1825	Thomas Billings, with Arthur Parker, buys 100 acres of the Manor of Leckhampton from Henry Norwood Trye.
1826	Grafton Street / Argyle Place / Grafton Road
1831	Park Place
1834	Lower Grafton Street / Ashford Road 1891
1835	Gloucesteshire Botanical, Horticultural & Zoological Society formed, buying 20 acres from Billings, who reserves 5 acres at north-east. He proposes a competition for the layout of the Gardens, which he wins.
1838	Opening of uncompleted Gardens
1841	Samuel Whitfield Daukes buys 20 acres from the Society, conserving 14 acres of woodland, and 6 acres as open space on the south.
1844	Andrew Taylor buys at auction the south part, selling to James Gilbertson.
1847	Fullwood House built
1850	Park Spa established by Billings on the north point of his 5 acre pleasure garden
1854	James Gilbertson builds Fulwood (Broadlands)
1882	Moorend Park Road developed
1897	Mrs McKnight-Crawford adds solarium at Fullwood House, and probably boathouse by lake.
1913	Ursuline Nuns establish ladies college at Fullwood.

1931	St. Mary's Training College
1939	Hostel wings added to Fullwood House.
1940	College evacuated to Llandrindod Wells, returning 1941.
1979	Amalgamation of St. Paul's and St. Mary's colleges
1990	College of Higher Education incorporating parts of GlosCAT, major building development and rationalization of outlier villas.
1999	Fullwood Villas
2001	Designation as University of Gloucestershire

Percentages of Statutory Listed and Local Listed Properties

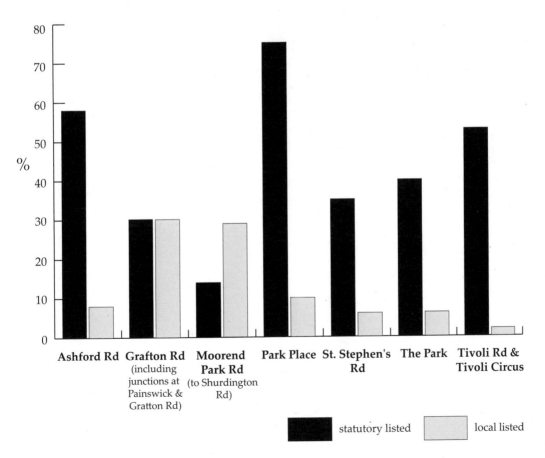

A Comparison between Cheltenham's earliest Parks

Pittville Park		The Park
Joseph Pitt, **lawyer**, buys 253 acres	1806	
Scheme for **100** acres walks, rides, lake (from Wyman's Brook) proposed 500-600 houses, **spa**, church	1824-30	
	1825	Thomas Billings, **lawyer**, buys **100** acres
John Forbes, **architect**		
Richard Ware, landscaper		
	1835	20 acres to Gloucestershire Botanical, Zoological and Horticultural Society, lake (Hatherley, Moorend Brooks) 5 acres for pleasure garden, proposed 43 houses
	1841	Sold to S.W. Daukes, **architect**. 14 acres arcadia, 6 acres sport
Pitt dies owing £50,000	1842	
	1844	Sold to A. Taylor
	1850	**Spa** at Billings' 5 acre pleasure garden
Park acquired by Borough	1891	
	1913	Ursuline Convent
	1931	St. Mary's College
	1990	Cheltenham & Gloucester College of Higher Education
	2001	University of Gloucestershire

First published in Great Britain in 2010 by Pallas Press

An Imprint of The University of Gloucestershire

© Copyright Original Texts & Illustrations Aylwin Sampson

The right of Mr Aylwin Sampson to be identified as the Author of the Work has been asserted by him in accordance with the Copyright, Designs and Patents Act 1988.

ISBN   1-86174-204-5

ISBN 13   978-1-86174-204-9

Printed and bound by MWL, South Wales

Pallas Press
University of Gloucestershire
The Park, Cheltenham
Gloucestershire
GL50 2RH
www.glos.ac.uk

CELEBRATING
175 Years
1834-2009
OF EDUCATING THE WORKFORCE